Jumbo Shrimp Guide

Wine Democracy

Forward: Stevie Kim
Project Curator: Richard Hough
Graphics: Miriam Ferrari
Featured Podcast Hosts: Cynthia Chaplin, Marc Millon, Polly Hammond, Steve Raye

Viale del Lavoro 8
37135 Verona
https://mammajumboshrimp.com/

ISBN: 978-88-946863-3-3

CONTENTS

Forward

by Stevie Kim

We are incredibly proud of the **Italian Wine Podcast**, our outstanding hosts, our fantastic guests, and the **consistently high quality of our content**. Since taking off in the early 2000s, interest in podcasting has grown exponentially, coinciding with the rise of smartphones, smart speakers and in-car entertainment systems. According to data published recently, over one-third (104 million) of Americans listen to podcasts regularly,[1] and 26% (80 million) of Americans are weekly podcast listeners.[2] During the COVID-19 emergency, which was to have significant implications for the wine sector more generally, **podcasting experienced unprecedented growth**, as audiences diversified (female listenership reached an all-time high in 2021). What's more, podcasting is a truly global phenomena, with Sweden leading the way for podcast consumption, followed by Ireland and Brazil, while North America and Asia Pacific have the highest number of listeners.

Against the backdrop of a global boom in the podcast medium, the **Italian Wine Podcast** has also experienced a remarkable surge in listener numbers (four million and

1. Buzzsprout, *Podcast Statistics and Data*, August 2022
2. Edison Research, *the infinite dial 2021*, March 2021

counting at the time of writing). It truly is a golden age for the podcast! But what does any of that have to do with **Wine Democracy**?

Well, we've been generating so much fantastic audio content that it seemed a shame that it was accessible in only one medium. Great books are often remade as films; great films spawn fantastic soundtracks; and amazing albums can inspire unforgettable live shows. So, we thought we'd try something similar with our podcasts, repurposing one medium into another, because we know that so many of you in the worldwide **Italian wine community** like nothing better than the feel of a brand-new book between your fingers.

While our podcast hosts each focus on a specific aspect of the international wine world (diversity, communications, food and wine and business), I've been able to take a more holistic approach, listening across the series for common threads and recurring themes. Of course, they all have the world of Italian wine at their heart, but I began to notice the emergence of another common theme – the theme I have come to know as **Wine Democracy**.

Of course, this common thread has emerged completely organically. It's not a subject our hosts (far less our guests) explicitly focused on and sometimes the correlation may seem ambiguous. Nonetheless, the theme (in my mind at least) was there - you just had to know what you were looking for!

While I had a relatively clear idea in my mind what **Wine Democracy** meant, I wanted to share my ideas with colleagues and flesh out the concept in a little more detail. So, I invited editorial colleagues and our team of podcast hosts to join the conversation and share their own ideas of what wine democracy means to them. We soon realized that concept was far wider than we had first understood - and even more topical than I had originally envisioned. In my opinion, **wine democracy is a theme for the ages**.

Having reached a willfully broad common understanding of what we meant by the term, I asked our hosts to identify podcast episodes from their back catalogues that they thought best conceptualized the idea of **Wine Democracy**. With well over a thousand episodes to choose from, this was a laborious exercise that required a certain degree of persuasion. Nonetheless, we soon found what we were looking for. A veritable treasure trove of content that was rich in quality and topicality.

Reconfiguring the audio content of a podcast into a book was another exercise that presented certain logistical and editorial challenges. With a blend of cutting-edge transcription technology and old-fashioned editorial grunt work, none of those challenges proved insurmountable.

The conversations we identified have been edited for length and clarity, while remaining true to the original spirit of the dialogue. For example, to remain focused on the issues particularly relevant to the theme of **Wine Democracy**, we've removed some of the "chit-chat" that makes the **Italian Wine Podcast** so engaging and edited out some of the "fluff" around the hosts' questioning. But don't worry, we've included a handy QR link to each of the podcast episodes, so you can quickly and easily immerse yourself in the full unedited audio experience of the **Italian Wine Podcast** as well!

As always, these publications are a truly collaborative effort and I'd like to take this opportunity to thank all my staff who have contributed, as well as our podcast hosts and guests for providing such rich, informed and erudite content.

A special thanks is due to Richard Hough, who sometimes partakes in various roles of il professore Attilio Scienza and, on this occasion, was the main lead in the content coordination, and to our podcasting team of Steve Raye, Cynthia Chaplin, Marc Millon, Polly Hammond and, last but not least, Professor Atillio Scienza. Also, a super-duper special mention to Joy Livingston, the Italian Wine Podcast producer, who tirelessly whips out a daily show (sometimes as many as ten episodes per week), and who had no idea what she herself was getting into when she took over from Jacob Melly and Margherita Andrenacci. And finally, a special thanks also goes to Lyka Caparas, our fantastic Clubhouse coordinator.

The Italian Wine Podcast began as a storytelling project dedicated to the Italian wine world. It started in March 2017 in the lead-up to two major Italian wine events: OperaWine and Vinitaly, and has since become an award-winning show, recognized as one of the most frequently listened-to wine podcasts out there. Since then, we've also launched an umbrella brand, Mamma Jumbo Shrimp, which encompasses the Italian Wine Podcast, its sister YouTube channel (@mammajumboshrimp), as well as the publishing arm which oversees the publication of books like this one.

When the Italian Wine Podcast was launched with Monty Waldin, the episodes were typically only 15/20 minutes long. Quite simply, we didn't think the audience had the patience for anything longer. That was until we started recording Ambassadors' Corner on Clubhouse during the COVID-19 pandemic and we realized that there was clearly an appetite for 'long-listen' content and more in-depth conversations.

The Italian Wine Podcast has gone from a mere 23k listens in 2017 to smashing four million listens at the time of writing. Although most of our content is in English, we also produce some of our content in Italian, most notably #everybodyneedsabitofscienza. This is partly to avoid diluting the authenticity of the content, but also to meet the demands of our rapidly expanding Italian audience.

So, if you're not already familiar the Italian Wine Podcast, here's a summary of what's on offer:

Monday - *Get US Market Ready with Italian Wine People* with Steve Raye (Business)
Tuesday - *Wine Food and Travel* with Marc Millon
Wednesday - *Voices* (diversity equity and inclusion) with Cynthia Chaplin
Thursday - *Clubhouse, Ambassador's Corner* with Stevie Kim
Wine2Wine Recorded Sessions, seminars from the annual business forum
Friday - *#everybodyneedsabitofscienza* with Professor Attilio Scienza
Saturday – *On the Road Edition* with Stevie Kim (Travel/Winery Visits)
Sunday – *Uncorked* with Polly Hammond (Wine Communication)

In addition to this full roster of outstanding programming, we also release a variety of ad hoc content including book narrations and special events.
Between our award-winning podcasts, stunning video content and informative books, whatever your role in the global wine community, we've got something for you.
Find us on Soundcloud, Spotify and iTunes, or wherever you get your podcasts.

Stevie Kim

@steviekim222
@italianwinepodcast
@mammajumboshrimp
@italianwinebook

Introduction

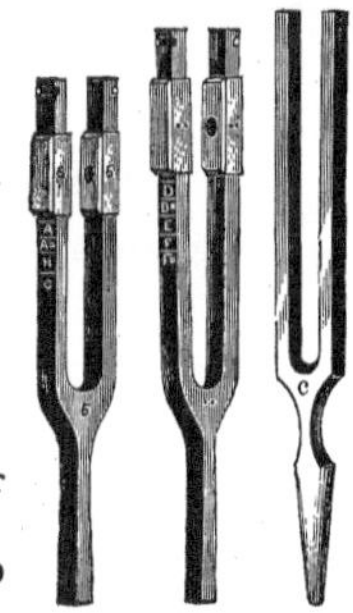

The concept of "**wine democracy**" is of great interest to us here at **Mamma Jumbo Shrimp**, but what does it mean?
Well, different things to different people (and we should know – we asked the hosts of **Italian Wine Podcast** and even they couldn't agree on a precise definition), but at its heart is the simple belief that wine should be more accessible.
If that sounds like we are advocating some kind of subsidy or price limit on wine, we're not! That's because accessibility isn't just about price (although excessive pricing may of course be a barrier to consumption for some). In fact, there are plenty of other obstacles, besides price, that deter consumers from engaging with and consuming wine.
Indeed, the concept of **wine democracy** touches upon education and recruitment, marketing and regulation, language, custom, practice and habit. In an industry not exactly known for its inclusivity, **wine democracy** is also concerned with equity and diversity. **Democratization of the wine sector means empowering those who have been excluded and developing policies that encourage wider participation in the industry** – a theme at the heart of Cynthia Chaplin's selection of conversations for inclusion in this publication, which also includes advice for young people from BIPOC and indigenous communities who want to enter the wine sector

from those with first-hand experience of that struggle.

Wine democracy is also concerned with the complex systems of legislation and regulation that govern the production, distribution and sale of alcoholic beverages in any given country, which, by design, restrict access to alcohol and, by definition, wine.

The world of wine is often perceived as elite and exclusive, while even the way wine is marketed, presented and served can seem incompatible with our modern tastes, habits and lifestyles. Canned wine, for example, offers convenience (portable and lightweight, ideal for parties, picnics or public transport), comes in smaller serve sizes so you don't have to buy a full bottle, and boasts significant environmental benefits too. Despite these advantages, there is still a profound stigma associated with drinking wine from a can, especially in the more traditional European markets. According to a 2022 report by Wine Intelligence, sales of canned wines have doubled since 2018, millennials account for 40% of the consumer base, while baby boomers make up just 8% of the canned wine market.[3]

Although this format is only just gaining a footing in the marketplace and volumes are currently small, wine in cans and other smaller-format bottles and packages are proving particularly popular with under 40s and are expected to grow significantly in the post-Covid context. Canned wine is just one example of an innovation that could open up (or democratize) wine consumption, and bring important environmental benefits too, but

3. Wine Intelligence, *Older, More Affluent Consumers Drive the US Wine Market*, https://www.wineintelligence.com/older-more-affluent-consumers-drive-the-us-wine-market/

the obstacles that stand in the way remain significant. Glass is perceived as more environmentally friendly than plastic, and glass bottles better reflect the values, tradition and quality of wine. They also look good on the table. Of course, the efficacy of glass in terms of weight, shipping costs and overall environmental impact is increasingly being challenged, with some industry figures even predicting that glass bottles could soon be a thing of the past.[4]

In fact, for many consumers, **the aesthetics and exclusivity of wine is part of its appeal**; the elegance of a bottle, the mystique of the label, the pomposity of the tasting notes, the elaborate theatre of popping the cork. Like collecting vinyl records, the expense and inconvenience are all part of the attraction! Indeed, wine has always been a prestige product and, in an age of instant depreciation, a rare example of a commodity that gains value with maturity.

Even the language we use around wine can be inaccessible, with a tendency among wine experts to use vague and abstract terminology. Elaborate, flowery flavor descriptors have become commonplace, and the vocabulary of wine is littered with terms ("terroir", "perlage", "minerality") which may seem familiar to insiders, but are, to many, incomprehensible and even off-putting.

While wine reviews and tasting notes can provide a useful source of information on the sensory properties of a particular wine (flavor, color, aroma etc.), its objective characteristics (color, grape type etc.), as well as

4. See for example, Prowein Magazine, *Wine in glass bottles – a no-brainer?*, https://www.prowein.com/en/Media_News/Magazine/All_articles/Wine_in_glass_bottles_%E2%80%93_a_no-brainer

an overall evaluation of wine's quality, there is an ongoing debate about the accessibility and even the utility of such reviews.[5] Furthermore, there is some evidence to suggest that wine consumers cannot align critics' descriptions of wines to the wine itself when they actually taste it. In fact, one academic study found that the consumer's ability to match the descriptions with the wines in question was no better than random![6]

In 2007, the eminent economist Richard E. Quandt conducted what he described in the *Journal of Wine Economics* as a **"bullshit-o-metric analysis"** of the vocabulary of wine descriptors, in which he reached the following remarkable conclusion:

"I think the wine trade is intrinsically bullshit-prone and therefore attracts bullshit artists. Some people are born bullshit artists, others learn to become bullshit artists, but if you fall into neither category and have ambitions in that direction, you may need my bullshit generating software."[7]

Although published in a serious academic journal by a serious professor of economics, the article clearly leans towards provocation and levity, rather than robust academic analysis, evidenced not least in its liberal employment of the term "bullshit", a delightfully unambiguous slang that you wouldn't normally expect to

5. Chenyu Yang, Jackson Barth, Duwani Katumullage and Jing Cao, *Wine Review Descriptors as Quality Predictors: Evidence from Language Processing Techniques*, "Journal of Wine Economics", Volume 17, 2022, 164-80

6. Weil, R. L. (2007). Debunking critics' wine words: Can amateurs distinguish the smell of asphalt from the taste of cherries? Journal of Wine Economics, 2(2), 136–144.

7. Quandt, R.E. (2007). *On wine bullshit: some new software.* Journal of Wine Economics, 2(2), 129–135.

grace the pages of a serious academic journal (excluding references and page headings, the term is repeated 35 times in the short seven-page article!). Nonetheless, Professor Quandt articulates a serious concern about the nature of wine evaluation and the shortcomings of the language used when we describe wine. Fifteen years later, the debate on whether wine reviews provide meaningful information on wine properties and quality is ongoing.

So, **the democratization of wine and the wine industry more generally is about increasing accessibility**. That's important, not just because it's the right thing to do - wine has a cultural value (as Professor Attilio Scienza likes to remind us) that belongs to us all - but also because there is a valid business case for doing so. **Diversity in the workforce**, as Dr Hoby Wedler eloquently explained in his conversation with Cynthia Chaplin, **is ultimately a bottom-line issue**, an observation repeated by Deborah Brenner and Josh Wand and others in conversation with Steve Raye. Though geographically there are still significant divergences in consumer behavior, global trends suggest that per capita wine consumption may now be lower than in previous years. On the other hand, wine consumption in general is expanding to increasingly diverse markets across a broader range of social classes and backgrounds. While in Portugal, Italy and France, the average per capita consumption is upwards of 45 liters a year, in China they consume barely a liter a head. Italy and France, which also happen to be the two biggest producers of wine, have seen consumption fall dramatically over the second half of the last century. In fact, the five biggest (by overall volume rather than per capita consumption) wine consuming countries in the world (USA, France, Italy, Germany and the UK) consume half of the world's wine (49%).[8]

Approaching the data from a slightly different perspective, continental Europe accounts for approximately 59% of the world's wine consumption. However, Europe, as the world's dominant consumer of wine, is a trend that has been in decline over the last 20 years, as global patterns of consumption evolve. In 2000, Europe accounted for 69% of global wine consumption, falling to 62% in 2012.[9] Meanwhile, on the other side of the globe in China, wine consumption fell by 17.4% in 2020, the third year in a row of declining consumption, a trend that is raising some doubts about China's place as "the next big market."[10]

On the face of it, these **imbalances in global wine consumption habits appear to represent a significant democratic deficit**, in which a few key players disproportionately dominate the global market. Might there be a democratic, as well as commercial, imperative to rebalancing the global wine market and giving smaller players a bigger voice?

Where wine is enthusiastically consumed, its cultural significance should not be underplayed, with certain

8. Forbes, *Wine Consumption In The World 2020 In Decline, A Detailed Look* https://www.forbes.com/sites/karlsson/2021/12/31/wine-consumption-in-the-world-2020-in-decline-a-detailed-look/
9. BK Wine Magazine, *The world's wine consumption 2000-2012*, https://www.bkwine.com/features/more/global-wine-consumption-2000-2012/
10. Forbes, *Wine Consumption In The World 2020 In Decline, A Detailed Look*, https://www.forbes.com/sites/karlsson/2021/12/31/wine-consumption-in-the-world-2020-in-decline-a-detailed-look/

wine producing regions even being recognized by UNESCO as World Heritage Sites. It is surely no coincidence that the civilizations of the western Mediterranean began to emerge from barbarism at around about the same time they learned to cultivate the olive and the vine.[11]

In addressing the theme of **wine democracy**, one must also consider **demographics**. Millennials (Generation Y – born between the early 1980s and the mid-1990s to early 2000s) aren't instinctively attracted to wine in the way their predecessors were. In fact, they display a distinct preference for premium spirits and craft beers, which they perceive as offering better value per serving. According to Silicon Valley Bank's State of the U.S. Wine Industry 2022 report, only 20% of millennials drink wine.[12] Generation Z (those born between the mid to late 1990s and the early 2010s), or "zoomers" as they are colloquially known, represent only around two percent of the wine consumer pool.[13]

Spiked seltzers and ready-to-drink cocktails are also gaining traction with this demographic and are expected to have an even greater impact over the next decade, representing an emerging challenge to the wine industry and how it engages with **younger consumers**.

This younger demographic isn't entirely bad news for the

11. An observation generally attributed to Thucydides, the Athenian historian and general.

12. Silicon Valley Bank Wine Division, *State of the US Wine Industry 2022*, https://www.svb.com/globalassets/trendsandinsights/reports/wine/svb-state-of-the-wine-industry-report-2022.pdf

13. See Mckinsey and Company, *'True Gen': Generation Z and its implications for companies*, 2018 https://www.mckinsey.com/industries/consumer-packaged-goods/our-insights/true-gen-generation-z-and-its-implications-for-companies

wine industry. By meeting their needs and aligning with their values, wine producers can open up a potentially lucrative market of discerning consumers – as Polly Hammond discovered in her conversation with Diva Giles, a young New Zealand bar owner who seems to have mastered the art of selling wine to young consumers.

As a cohort of consumers, Generation Z values authenticity, seeks greater variety, engages with brands and responds to personalized marketing. They are interested in provenance and sustainability and favor word-of-mouth recommendations. They are digital natives with significant purchasing power. They make impulse purchases and value experiences over things. While of course, such characteristics are, by definition, generalizations, and some may even seem contradictory, there is no doubt that these are characteristics that the wine sector can work with.

By-appointment tastings are one way of giving young consumers the experiences they crave, while off-property experiences can also be used to attract consumers unable to visit a winery in person. For this younger generation, consumption is about access rather than possession, the expression of individual identity rather than mass conformity, and reflects an **increasing awareness and empathy for ethical considerations.**[14]

With the wine industry struggling to engage a younger audience, particularly in places like America, where wine is no longer as popular with consumers as it once

14. McKinsey & Company *'True Gen': Generation Z and its implications for companies*, https://www.mckinsey.com/industries/consumer-packaged-goods/our-insights/true-gen-generation-z-and-its-implications-for-companies

was, **a process of "democratization" may actually help the industry to unlock those hard-to-reach markets**. How it engages with these values in the future will determine its success in reaching the next generation of wine consumer, but, according to some analysis, the industry has shown little willingness to adapt its marketing approach to attract or retain these younger, health-conscious, multicultural consumers.[15]

Drinking less but better is a trend that is evident across all demographic cohorts, not just the young. While this "premiumization" of the market will inevitably favor the premium segment, it also raises questions around the need to "democratize" the sector. Premium wines, of course, come with a certain price point and producers will have to figure out how to produce their wine for an entry-level consumer. Without a viable "on-ramp", the wine sector may be left behind, an observation echoed in the 2022 Silicon Valley Bank report.

Of course, the ongoing **impact and aftermath of the COVID-19 pandemic** looms large over any discussion of the trends and issues currently facing the wine sector. While many analysts predicted that consumers would celebrate in 2021, making up for the many postponed life events that the pandemic necessitated by opening a bottle of bubbles, in the American market, at least, wine didn't benefit from the reopening as much as spirits did. That, also, is something that the industry needs to consider.

One of the big things prosecco has successfully done is

15. Silicon Valley Bank Wine Division, *State of the US Wine Industry 2022* (page 11) https://www.svb.com/globalassets/trendsandinsights/reports/wine/svb-state-of-the-wine-industry-report-2022.pdf

change the perception of sparkling wine from a "celebratory" option only, to an everyday choice.

Though the American market ultimately proved resilient and agile in the face of everything the last couple of years has thrown at it (not just COVID, but also supply chain issues and price inflation), and 2021 was objectively a "good" year for the U.S. wine industry,[16] longer term trends, including falling interest in wine among younger consumers and the approaching retirement and falling consumption habits of baby boomers, means that **engaging with new markets has never been more important**.

If **America remains the ultimate market to crack** (in 2021 Italian wine export sales exceeded 1.72 billion euros accounting for over 24% of total exports, according to figures published by the Italian National Institute of Statistics), Steve Raye has described navigating its three-tier system as like peeling an onion - every time you peel a layer, there's another one underneath that makes you want to cry! In America and beyond, bureaucracy and trade barriers remain a significant barrier to those wishing to access markets and, therefore, to the "democratization" of the wine industry.

Technology has an important role to play breaking down these barriers, a theme that Steve Raye has been particularly assiduous in exploring in his podcast series Get U.S. Market Ready with Italian Wine People. Wineries are increasingly taking **data-driven approaches** and an increasing number of **sophisticated digital plat-**

16. See, for example, Silicon Valley Bank Wine Division, *State of the US Wine Industry 2022* https://www.svb.com/globalassets/trendsandinsights/reports/wine/svb-state-of-the-wine-industry-report-2022.pdf

forms are now available to promote and sell wine online. This improved access to data and technology has significant implications for small and medium-sized enterprises. Indeed, Steve has highlighted the experience of the Liquor Fountain, a single store seller in Los Angeles, which has leveraged such technology to engage more effectively with their online customers (**Italian Wine Podcast**, episode 735).

Another example of how technological innovation can drive democratization comes in the form of powerful new **search engines** like Wine-Searcher. As Don Kavanagh, editor of Wine-Searcher, explained:

"We are just trying to put as much information into the hands of the ultimate buyer as possible."

Of course, technology like this relies on the quality and accessibility of the information at its disposal, a point that Steve Raye probed in his conversation with Don Kavanagh. More generally, **access to information** is another key theme in the "democracy" discussion.

Social media also has an increasingly important role to play in relation to the democratization of wine, particularly for young consumers. Writing recently in Harpers Wine & Spirit magazine, Guy Woodward, Director of the International Wine & Spirit Competition and Club Oenologique, argued that while Twitter had "opened up the wine world to hobbyists and amateurs in what was, at first, a largely informed, democratic debate," Instagram has succeeded in "opening up the previously distant, elitist wine world to a new market, often by showcasing more affordable wines in a more personal manner." On the other hand, Woodward observed:

"without informed critical judgement, the content becomes one big – but unlabeled – ad for those brands with the biggest PR budgets".[17] So, **social media** is important, but it's no silver bullet.

Of course, **wine education** also has a crucial role to play, particularly in relation to creating a more standardized approach to wine tasting, but also in helping consumers to make informed and critical judgements. This is a point that was highlighted by Nicole Brassard Jordan, the Deputy Commissioner of the New Hampshire Liquor Commission, when she explained to Steve Raye the importance of educational training for her staff to help them better inform the consumer. Indeed, education is important for consumers, but also for those in the industry, or those seeking to enter it, and not just wine specific education, but also how the industry works more generally.

Even with a standardized vocabulary, tasting wine is a highly subjective experience. As Harold McGee's acclaimed book *Nose Dive* explains, our aromatic referents are culturally specific. Asian consumers, for example, have completely different sensory reference points to their European counterparts, while the Chinese language has no word for "sour" or "acidic." We must be mindful, then, of **cultural and linguistic anomalies** (if we may call them such) when discussing wine in a global context, as the overlapping concepts of globalization and democratization present new challenges to an old trade, a point explicitly made by Chinedu Rosa, who grew up in Lagos, in her conversation with Polly Hammond.

17. Harpers Wine & Spirt, Guy Woodward: Wine's 'social experts' https://harpers.co.uk/news/fullstory.php/aid/30227/Guy-Woodward:_Wine_s__social_experts__.html

One way to confront the obfuscating nature of modern wine-speak is to take **a more scientific approach**, thinking of flavors in terms of chemistry rather than gastronomy. That's certainly an approach that the **Vinitaly International Academy** (VIA) is pioneering in its program of Italian wine education courses. Writing recently in Meininger's Wine Business International, IWA faculty member Sarah Heller MW argued that communicating about wine effectively requires us to consciously adopt different registers for different audiences. Indeed, working with faculty colleagues, VIA has decided to teach the compounds that are likely behind varietal aromas, while ultimately prioritizing commonly understood descriptors like herbs, fruit and flowers.[18]

In the workplace, the wine industry needs to be more creative about **diversity in the hiring process**. Josh Wand, Founder & Motivator in Chief of BevForce, explained how working practices were changing in the context of **COVID-19**, with attitudes and approaches towards new practices like **home and hybrid working** slowly beginning to shift, presenting opportunities for the wine sector to diversify its workforce, with leadership coaching and mentoring also playing increasingly important roles. Already, as we move forward in the new "post-Covid" reality, many of those emerging practices are now well-established.

Meanwhile, facing up to **the climate emergency** will require unprecedented levels of cooperation and sacrifice at a local, national and international level, one of many

18. Meininger's Wine Business International, *Guest feature: Sarah Heller MW on the Language of Wine*, https://www.wine-business-international.com/wine/guest-feature-sarah-heller-mw-language-wine

themes explored in the conversation between Cyntia Chaplin and Elaine Chukan Brown. With increasing climate impacts from drought, fire, low soil moisture and declining water reserves, there will be even more pressure for agriculture and academia to share resources and expertise. It will be the ultimate test of the industry's "democratic" principles and may even require us to accept some decidedly undemocratic, even draconian, measures. But, if the industry, and indeed the planet itself, is going to survive the existential crisis that the climate emergency represents, solutions must also come from within the sector itself – not least from those at the coalface.Beyond climate change, **wine democracy** is also concerned with **the preservation and protection of vulnerable ecosystems and fragile cultures**. This is a recurring theme that Marc Millon has explored in his conversations with wine producers from across Italy. From the lagoons of Venice to the remote vineyards of the Sardinian interior, co-operation and partnership are vital if the future of this priceless cultural patrimony is to be preserved. As always in Italy, the need to innovate and modernize must be balanced against the need to protect and preserve.

So, with the democratization of the wine industry becoming an increasingly pressing issue, with the potential to unlock many of the big issues currently facing the sector, we decided to approach some of the people who know the industry best – our **Italian Wine Podcast** hosts – and get their views on the subject. Of course, they all approach the topic from a slightly different perspective, but what follows is a series of edited transcripts of some truly fascinating conversations with producers and distributors, educators and importers, influencers, sommeliers, and Masters of Wine, all of whom have confronted and overcome challenges in their personal and professional lives, emerging, in one way or another, as **true champions of wine democracy**.

Voices

CYNTHIA CHAPLIN

Introduction

“Democracy” generally refers to rule by the people. A truly representative democracy should incorporate all members of society, regardless of their numbers, and all creeds, philosophies and beliefs should coexist within the democracy despite their inherent differences.

Taking this definition and loosely draping it over the global wine sector, my definition of “Wine Democracy” is one that aspires to an inclusive industry, encouraging language and references that are drawn from all cultures, all levels of experience, and all roles within the sector. For me, wine democracy would also include all types of wine and all wine grapes, all methods of vinification and packaging, all methods of communication, marketing and education.

Wine democracy should include all ages of consumers and professionals, all people without specifying gender, race or cultural background; in fact, my vision of wine democracy is of a constantly lengthening table with an endless supply of seats, welcoming everyone who wishes to enjoy wine, learn about wine, or become a professional in any area of the sector. No wine, however banal or avant-garde, and no person, however new to the field or possessing particular perspectives, should be excluded or discouraged.

A true wine democracy would be a space where all wines and all people are encouraged to improve, to learn, to be the best at whatever role, large or small, they choose in the global wine industry. There should be no more "bad wine", rather, acceptance of wines that are intentionally of a lower quality and appropriate for bulk wine consumers, blending, mixing for cocktails, and so on. Exalted wines should, of course, retain their well-earned reputations, but they should not be seen as beyond the reach of those who are new to the wine world. All wines should be accessible to all people, if not financially accessible, then at least educationally and informationally accessible. Wine language should not exclude, but seek to engage an increasingly wider audience, particularly given the fact that the global pandemic, logistical challenges, decreasing wine consumption in younger drinkers, and the challenges facing the world in terms of recession, climate change, and geopolitical aggression have all contributed to reduced wine consumption around the world.

A true wine democracy would not judge the choices of winemakers nor wine drinkers, but would instead use data and storytelling to demonstrate that wine is a product that historically offers something for everyone, never more so than at this moment in time.

Conversation I

EPISODE 862

ELAINE CHUKAN BROWN

The audio

The issues

I chose this episode because Elaine is from an indigenous community that is unfamiliar to many people. Elaine shares their experience of overcoming obstacles to their own education, then demonstrates how they became an inclusive educator their self. Their understanding of the connection between education, language, sustainability and inclusion is profound and they focus on those topics in every aspect of their work. This conversation also addressed the climate emergency, with some concrete examples of how the industry is confronting the issue.

The guest

Elaine Chukan Brown is indigenous from Alaska. Their families originated in the Norton Sound region of Alaska, and their grandmother helped instigate the Alaskan native heritage preservation movement in the state. Elaine is now based in Sonoma, where they serve as a writer, a speaker, and an educator specializing in wine and personal empowerment and social justice. They've won huge acclaim for their Hawk WakaWaka wine reviews and, after several years as an American specialist wine reviewer for Jancis Robinson, Elaine was appointed executive editor (US) of Jancisrobinson.com in 2022.

The conversation

ECB: My dad's side is from Norton Sound, which is on the western coast of Alaska, and my family on that side is Iñupiat, which is a Northern Alaskan Inuit group. My mom's side is from the Bristol Bay region, and her side is Unangan Sugpiaq, so again, broadly speaking, an Inuit group. The point is these are all coastal water peoples of Alaska.

I still have obstacles because of being indigenous. In elementary school I was regularly pulled from class to go to special programs just for indigenous kids. That would sometimes mean I was missing learning how to read or studying basic math and things like that. It's a challenge for schools when they're trying to create programs specially geared towards certain kinds of groups or certain kinds of needs. Sometimes they're inadvertently causing kids to miss the things everyone else is getting. I had great grades. I was regularly in honors classes before high school but, even so, I had counsellors try to keep me from advanced classes that I wanted to take because they thought they were too hard for indigenous kids.

In high school, I had a mini protest and I refused to leave the scheduling office until they gave me the courses I said I wanted. Thankfully that finally worked, but then going into graduate school, in some of the courses I took we would be studying communication and cultural questions, and the materials we would be reading would seem too narrow to me and, if I raised examples from my cultural background, I actually had one professor tell me, "Well, those examples aren't real."

I was raised by people who understood these things are simply true. These things just happen and we keep focused on what it is we intend to do. I was very much raised with that sort of mindset. It's ultimately been a big service for me.

CC: Wine Industry Network named you one of the Most Inspiring People in Wine in 2019 and you were Wine Communicator of the Year in 2020. You've been known to say that your primary goal is always to witness the life in front of you, be it the person or the glass. How are you achieving that goal in your work as a communicator?

ECB: My first job is to listen. Listening, as funny as it might sound, is a full body activity. My attention, if I'm meeting with a producer or viticulturist or sommelier or someone otherwise working in wine or even more broadly, of course, just interacting with people, my job is quite simply to be present. Listening is not just about using your ears, it's very much about overall observation. That's what I mean when I say it's a full body activity. My job is to be observant, and I can't write a piece or speak to a topic in a seminar, for example, until I really have done that work of careful observation and listening first, because I really want to understand where a person is coming from, what is influencing the region, to what extent is the wine that I'm drinking informed by the growing conditions of the place, the demands of that vintage, the people making it and history they've come from?

All of these things factor into the final expression in a glass of wine, and I'm there to try to observe all these factors and tease out the pieces I can communicate clearly. Also, I've chosen this job, I've worked really hard to get to where I am now, but that also means I'm the person with the luxury of all that, of that time with these people that make our wine. I know a lot of wine lovers would love to have that time with producers and travel the world getting to know wine as I have done, so I really see that as my second duty.

As I said, first I want to observe and listen to understand, and then I ask myself how can I communicate this clearly in a way that offers something to the reader or the audience while also respecting those people that gave me their time so that I could understand.

Since before I started in wine, I've been having conversations about social equity and responsibility to our communities. Once I stepped into wine, that was always braided into my work, it's always been there.

A number of producers actually brought up work that I've done previously and I found out the region I was in had actually done a lot of diversity, equity and inclusion (DEI) training in the previous several months across their industry and actually sent links to several talks I gave to two producers I was going to visit so that they were more aware.

It's interesting to witness this because it says so much

about how the people we choose to elevate into leadership positions really are influencing all of us, whether they're directly trying to or not. Just because I have this fancy new title, the fact that I've been doing work on diversity and also on climate action for years now is already influencing people I meet before I even get there. That's a really interesting experience for me to see. Then, more overtly of course, I'm always keeping an eye out for how these efforts being made by other people working on climate action or social responsibility, how does that inform stories that are relevant to the site too.

CC: **You led a series called Rooted for Good that was sponsored by the Jackson family, which was all about climate action and social justice. Can you explain that project to our listeners?**

ECB: Jackson Family Wines own quite a few different wineries, many of them are quite small niche brands. They also own a good number of brands and vineyards all up and down the West Coast as well as elsewhere. They have spent quite a lot of time, well over fifteen years now, trying to systematically increase their sustainability efforts. They were founded with that kind of interest, but of course we as a culture and an industry, our understanding of what it means to do that has increased so much as well. They formed a division in their company just devoted to sustainability and they started measuring their own carbon footprint, their water usage, their power usage, all of these things. Then, over time, they also created an employee task force so that problem solving could really come from within. How do we improve on any of these efforts? Employees actually working with washing barrels or the cellar or irrigation and vineyards or any of these things, they're the ones that know where improvements could be made. That was how the effort was designed, bringing employees together to brainstorm.

Just last year they announced this initiative that they call Rooted for Good. It's a ten-year commitment to cut their carbon footprint in half, to significantly decrease water usage and improve water management, while also supporting healthy habitats, and they're moving their entire fleet to electric over time. All these things can only happen over time, right?

Then, of course, they have a social responsibility component too. They do a lot to support their own employees, but also to make it possible for their employees to support their own communities. I got brought in because they have an interest in figuring out how do we best communicate this effort in a way that's not about promoting them as much as sharing what they're learning. They reached out to me to see if I would be willing to help them design a webinar of some sort. I said I would be interested in doing this if we could make it a pretty robust, thorough, educational series where, of course, Jackson family representatives would be present so we could use them as a case study on these topics, but they wouldn't be the focus.

I wasn't sure if they would be willing to do that, but right away they said, wow, that's exactly what we want. So, I spent the first half of the year getting really knowledgeable about how the carbon cycle works, how water management and rainfall informed habitat preservation and wild reservoirs and all these different technical things. There was a lot of work on that side.

I spent half a year reading a lot of scientific papers, getting to know what Jackson Family was actually doing, but also interviewing scientists, researchers, government leaders, lots of different people, and then I came back to the team with the five-webinar design and suggestions on what kinds of people we would want to interview for each and what the conversations could look like depending on who we chose.

Then we worked together to invite experts from around the world. We did a five-part series. The first was on the carbon cycle. We also brought in a glass supplier to interview them on how we can reduce the carbon impact from packaging and transportation.

In that particular episode, we had climate scientist Kimberley Nicholas, originally from California but now based in Sweden. Her book, *Under the Sky We Make*, is something I strongly recommend just because it gives you the facts that you need to know, but also in a way that is encouraging and very clear and understandable. We were also able to interview a representative from the United Nations on that episode, which was pretty incredible. For the second episode, we moved into habitat restoration and water management and looked at how practices in our wineries and vineyards can be co-supported with the surrounding environment as well.

That one ended up in some ways being the most California-focused because it's such a stress point here, but it's really relevant worldwide. Some of the details shift, of course, depending on your conditions, but there's a lot of important information there. Then we looked at soil health and regenerative farming. That was one of our most popular episodes. People are really interested in that work right now, which was cool to see.

In the fourth episode, we looked at social responsibility. How can we use programs to increase and improve employee engagement so that the support employees need really are being shown and generated by them, and the company can respond in that way, and then use that as a perspective on how to improve diversity efforts as well, but in a way that's not just about a company, but about the company's place in its surrounding communities.

In that fourth episode, we were able to bring in Rob Symington, from the Symington Family Estates, and talk about the work they're doing in Portugal and the Douro, and then also here in Napa Valley. Beth Milliken from Spottswoode was able to talk about the work they're doing and forming their estate-based winery as well. The series happened over several months and it's been interesting to see the effect of that as well.

On the trip I was just on, it turned out a number of people had watched it live as it was happening and talked about how it changed some of the work that they're doing in their wineries and vineyards, too, which is exciting and again with the goal it was not about promoting Jackson Family, though I believe the effort they're making is super important and really can act as a guide for others, it was really about trying to offer insight that can benefit all of us as an industry.

CC: The project also highlights how valuable it is to engage with the people who work for you and get them

vested in what you're doing and make use of their experience and opinions in a meaningful way.
ECB: The truth is, they're the people that make the process happen. A company leader might have the most insightful, forward-thinking ideas in the world, but if the people they work with or who work for them don't believe in it too, those ideas are not going to come to fruition. Our employees are who make our work happen, so they have to be engaged in that kind of way. The more we can think from that perspective, how do we work together as a team, the more quickly we can reach our goals.
CC: Tell us about Hawk WakaWaka, your wine reviews and Instagram persona.
ECB: When I got started in wine I was still in my academic career and so I needed professional anonymity. I decided, if I'm going to make up a name, I might as well make up a really good one. Honestly, from my teens, some people have called me Hawk, it was a nickname, so that's where that part comes from.
The full length of the original name was Lily Elaine Hawk WakaWaka. The first three parts of the name Lily, Elaine and Hawk, were all either literally my name or nicknames I'd had. Anyone who has known me long enough would recognize at least two of those three. Just like great wine, you need a good finish and so Lily Elaine Hawk WakaWaka. That brings the flourish at the end.
The original idea was I wanted a name that anyone who knew me well enough would realize, oh my gosh, it has to be Elaine, but anyone that didn't know me would

see no natural tie to my actual name. Then, at the same time, I wanted a name that was simultaneously ridiculous, yet had gravitas. So, Lily Elaine Hawk WakaWaka is quite a name!

Once I realized the kind of name I wanted, that name immediately came to mind, and I started laughing. I realized, there you go, that's the name. If I'm laughing because of it, it works. With online limits, it got shortened to Hawk WakaWaka. Without my realizing in advance that this would be true, it turned out using this ridiculous name Hawk WakaWaka actually helped my career. That was never the plan, I just needed a name I enjoyed. It's the kind of name that when people see it, they say, what on earth is that? Click, and they follow the link, so I think it in some ways led to more readership and more attention.

I've been doing this in wine now for about ten years, but the first half of that people mostly knew me as Hawk WakaWaka and didn't know who Elaine Chukan Brown was.

Then it started to shift to where people would know both. Now it's flipped so that people know who Elaine Chukan Brown is and have no idea what Hawk Wak aWaka is. It's fun. Occasionally, I'll bump into someone I haven't met before, but they've known me since Hawk WakaWaka. I got started doing these quirky drawings, and that's how they remember me. It turned out to be kind of an insight into how someone knows me too.

I originally got started in wine by drawing my tasting notes instead of writing them. In the middle of 2011, when I started doing this, visual tasting notes had not been published before. It's so fascinating now, eleven years later, to see people have come up with so many creative interpretations of communicating wine visually.When I started, that was not a thing. We were, I think, really at this turning point where there was this struggle to find a new way to communicate and things like Instagram were just starting to gain a foothold, they were not as well formed as now.

I was into wine. I had friends that loved wine but were intimidated and I wanted to come up with a way of making it feel simpler for them, more approachable.

I enjoyed drawing and just suddenly had this moment where I was like, "oh my God", I could draw my tasting notes. If I do that well, it'll just make sense, because the thing about a visual input is the picture is worth a thousand words. You see it and you understand, it doesn't have to be spelled out in words. I think that's the thing about wine, too. When we taste it, if we like it, we just do, it doesn't have to be spelled out, but traditional wine communication is all about talking, talking, talking!

CC: I know you're devoting a lot of time and energy to mentoring young people and other BIPOC and indigenous people. What advice would you have for a young person from those communities who wants to enter the wine sector now? What lessons and wisdom can you pass along from your own experience?

ECB: The most important thing is to try to connect with other people and build a community and recognize it takes time to do that. It's the strongest form of support any of us will find as we navigate our way through wine. The wine industry is quirky. It's a challenge. There are so many good people in wine and yet there's so many tiny little companies and little individual regions. In a lot of ways, the industry is really bifurcated. There are all these tiny parts that have tenuous links between them. As a person coming into the industry, that can be so intimidating and difficult and just opaque to try to figure out how to navigate. The most important thing is to remember it takes time and to find those channels of support that will help give you someone to lean on or people to get help and guidance from.

The thing to say is that wine was not hard to learn, the wine industry is what was challenging.

They're really different skill sets, and I think sometimes we fail to admit that. There's a lot of scholarships and wine specific education that's available now, thankfully, but it's important for all of us to remember that the wine education that has been available doesn't usually cover how the industry works.

CC: You started the Diversity in Wine Leadership Forum in 2020 with Maryam Ahmed. What's the forum up to these days?

ECB: Maryam Ahmed came up with the idea of helping to connect these different organizations in wine working on diversity efforts. Then Maryam came to talk to me, and I said this is a great idea, but we need to remember that diversity doesn't have traction unless it's focused on equity too. The two of us came together and we initially started by helping to bring together organizations working on diversity. The idea was, look, we're going to get tired, any one of us can't solve this, it's so big, we need to find ways to problem solve together, to collaborate, to share insights. So, we initially started that way, and then we realized that there was actually a big interest. People wanted to know what we were doing and wanted to have the opportunity to learn themselves. We then progressed into creating a central resource for people to find these organizations and now also offer educational series for people wanting to learn how to do better and support diversity efforts more broadly.

CC: How do you see the U.S. wine sector in contrast to other wine producing places around the world?

One of the things that's unique about the U.S. is that our biggest market is also where we make the wine, and that cannot be overlooked. That in so many ways defines the difference between U.S. wine and any other part of the world. There are great advantages with that economically, of course, though sometimes that can also stunt a region or producer's progress. Sometimes, if it's easy to sell, you don't have to push as hard to elevate your work. That said, of course, there are incredible producers here really devoted to elevating their work and their quality, and so many people leading the way in that. The fact that we can make and sell the wine in one place is not just an economic impact, it's a big cultural impact as well.

The takeaway

> **"Create community and empower employees to lead innovation within the workplace."**

Conversation II

EPISODE 834 - PHIL LONG

The audio

The issues

For me, this episode really represents a triumph over prejudice, challenge, and loss, as well as a huge generosity of spirit, all rolled up into "a big bowl of jelly beans". Only Phil Long could make this analogy work.

The guest

Phil Long is the President of the Association of African American Vintners and the founder of Longevity Wines, which is in Livermore Valley in Northern California. He started the company in 2002 in his garage with his late wife Debra and they grew the business together, opening their own facility in 2008. Now Phil is partnering with Bronco Wine Company with facilities and national distribution across the USA.

The conversation

CC: Wine was not your first career path. You have an architecture degree from Cal Poly in Pomona, and you said you weren't even aware that wine *was* a career path. So, how did you discover wine and get into the business?

PL: Yes, that's totally true. The guys we called "Aggies" back in college, they were the guys with cowboy hats and cowboy boots that had a little animal stench to them. I thought, wow, that's what you do with animals. But those were the guys that were growing grapes and I had no idea. Full circle, going to Cal Poly Pomona and earning my degree, now the university library is archiving its only graduate's wine brand, Longevity, which is interesting, again, coming full circle.

The journey you take as you grow up, you start sampling wine and enjoying wine. You have friends that have wine and invite you over. Debra and I just started to become more aware of it. In Southern California wine is basically just a commodity. It's something you get at a restaurant or the grocery store and take home. When we relocated to Northern California, we realized that wine is part of the fabric of life here. You literally can't drive in any direction without ending up in wine country. As we explored our surroundings every weekend, we found ourselves in wine country, and that interest, passion, lifestyle, it just grew on us. We started making a little wine in the garage just for fun, just as a couple's hobby. That's how it started.

CC: I'm guessing the reality of it wasn't the easiest row to hoe, going from making wine in your garage to ramping up to the production that you have now. What was the development process like for you and Debra in the early days?

PL: Yes, that's so much a part of the story. I had a couple of really great mentors in the Valley that helped me along. That first vintage that Debra and I made wine in the garage, we made 30 gallons of Syrah. For nine months you covet these 30 gallons, thinking it's the greatest gift to mankind, but somewhere along the line you realize it's just total crap.

I can say that now. The justification for making more was, well, I made it in the wrong size barrel. You got to make it in the 60-gallon barrel, not a 30-gallon barrel. Then you've got to get a rack. Well, a rack holds two. Look, they stack too.

So, it just snowballed into having a barrel room in the garage which held twelve barrels and at some point we just said, look, we've got to do something. At the same time, we obtained our wholesale distributors license and started an online based wine club and literally visited hundreds and hundreds of wineries here in California. That's so much the story of going into wineries, seeing how we were treated [as a bi-racial couple], seeing how people did things.

We just learned early on that we wanted to create an immersive tasting experience for everyone. There were times we walked in a tasting room and they didn't even acknowledge that we were even in there. There was one time I walked into a tasting room by myself, and there were no customers there, and the two people behind the counter were too busy trying to help a customer on the phone to even acknowledge I walked through the door.

This was in the early 2000s or mid 2000s, which is remarkable. But we used those experiences to learn from and figure out who we wanted to be and finally opened our own tasting room facility and production facility in the Livermore Valley in 2008. We started with the vintage of 500 cases in 2008, and then we grew by 500 cases a year and it wasn't about what fruit we wanted to get, it was what fruit we could get, either by budget or availability.

The cool thing is, some of those vineyards we started with, we now manage with our own vineyard manager because we take all the fruit and we've just grown to that degree.

CC: You had a serious accident back in the day. A barrel fell from the top of a four-barrel high stack and landed on your head, and you spent several months in rehab. A quote from you that I read really stood out to me. You said, "As long as I can still taste, I think we should move forward". That shows a lot of inherent strength and persistence, same things we want in our wine. But what came out of that period, how did you move forward after that accident? It sounds like it was pretty grave.

PL: It was pretty ugly because it happened on a Sunday morning at the winery by myself, the radio blasting, wine pump running, and I was jockeying around this stack of barrels in it. It was an empty barrel, but an empty barrel from 16ft high at 125 pounds, hitting you square on the head before you even know it's off the rack is pretty horrendous.

Basically, it compressed my spinal cord so that any signals going below my neck were non-existent. I was either going to lay there and bleed to death or somebody was going to find me. Luckily, Debra found me. I was in ICU for four or five days and then in-house rehab for three weeks and two days, then outpatient rehab for probably a year after that.

I'm still not 100%. I have some dexterity issues, but you're right at the point where you're in rehab and you're in a wheelchair and you can't feed yourself or walk, you start looking at options and decisions. The bottom line is, as long as I have a palate and I can taste and I have the ability to evaluate and even tell other people what to do, we decided to move forward. Inevitably, I'm quite normal. I say I'm not 100%. I'm 97%, so all is good in that range.

CC: I want to talk about the name of your winery.

PL: When Debra and I were making wine in the garage, it would just be us. It was just something we did together and had fun and we could share with friends. When we first started thinking about a winery name, I said, well, what do you think of Long Family Cellars? And she just kind of stopped and turned and looked at me and said, what other family do you see cleaning up this crap? Yeah, you got a point. So, she came up with the name Longevity, and we named our first wine, which was a GSM, Longevity.

The name just stuck, and we took the name Longevity for the winery and then we had to rename that wine, so that's become a Debraveée which is short for Debra's Cuvée. So, yeah, it's been Longevity ever since. As for the heart on the label, I would give Debra these glass hearts every Valentine's Day, and she amassed a huge collection of hearts and heart clothing and heart pictures on the wall, so when we rebranded somewhere around 2009, I designed the heart that's on the label. It included more hearts, grapevines and grapes, because it truly represented who Debra and I were at the time. It represented our life, our love, all of it. That's what became the iconic label that's been seen on dozens and dozens of TV shows here in the US. Then, unfortunately, as you said, she was diagnosed with stage four pancreatic cancer in 2016. I got to take her with me, at least for the first [tattoo] sitting, because there were many sittings. My left arm is the full sleeve of that heart from the middle of my wrist to my elbow.

We started this together and I made her the promise that we were going to finish this together. So, family run business. I get to tell the story of Debra every day, which I'm blessed to be able to do, and that keeps me going. The sad part is that she knew what was happening, what was in the process of happening. Unfortunately, she's not here to experience the benefits from that, but it's my job now to keep her memory alive and I made her the promise that the mosaic of her picture at the winery is never coming down, and I'm going to keep that promise. The interesting thing, the TV exposure [Big Little Lies, Big Bang Theory, Frankie and Grace,] was part of Debra and I's plan to gain more brand awareness outside of our own regional reach. It's not like people come flocking to your website to buy your wine. It's just a piece of the branding puzzle. You've got to have all those pieces together. What I will say, what I think it did do for us, that national exposure, I believe, helped us gain the partnership with Bronco Wine Company, among many other things. That step into the national spotlight definitely helped the process.

CC: The partnership is interesting: you're making your wines with fruit from the Franzia family, and you're using Bronco's state of the art zero waste facility in Ceres in California, and you're doing a lot of things that are quite sustainable as well. You've got a new closure method called the Helix that's 100% recyclable. What's coming along the pipeline for Longevity?

PL: Debra and I started when it was just the little family, which it still is just a family-owned entity. Our goal was to get to somewhere between 3000 and 3500 cases a year. Partnering with Bronco, first of all, as a winemaker, it's a ton of fun because, trust me, their spice rack is a whole lot larger than mine. Going to blend wines in their lab, which I have done with my son, is a lot of fun because you just have access to so much more.

That part of the journey is great. This partnership, they have enough belief in me that basically they just gave me the keys to the winery and said, "go get it". So, we strategically plan what we're going to release and when we're going to release it. When we started, nationally we only had a Chardonnay and a Cabernet. Of course, we released those in March 2020 - I don't need to remind anybody what that time was.

We got through 2020. It was the worst time! To that line up, we've added a rosé of Pinot Noir known as Debra's Cuvée which I'm happy to carry that name on. Since then, we've also added two Phil Long Reserve wines, a Napa Valley Cabernet Sauvignon and Sonoma Valley Cabernet Sauvignon. We have a private label wine going into a very large retailer here in the spring. We will be releasing Albariño in the main line up before the end of the year. We are also working on two sparkling. So, that's what's coming up.

CC: That's huge growth! Do you see yourself ever becoming a vineyard owner or are you going to be happy with buying in grapes?

PL: No, it's interesting. Debra and I, we always had the goal of what we called the compound, which is vineyard, winery, home for my son and his family. The compound is still on the horizon. We're not quite there yet but going from 500 cases to the ultimate goal of a million cases a year, I think we'll get there. It's family, it's gathering, it's chickens, it's dogs, it's cats. It's just a comfortable lifestyle where everyone can be together and be about family, work together, play together and enjoy each other. We're just not here that long.

CC: You became President of the Association of African American Vintners in 2020 and Longevity is a certified minority owned business as well. You've said you never wanted to be a "black winemaker", but now you've become a spokesperson for African American winemaking in the industry. How do you view this role? What are your goals for AAAV?

PL: Just like I never wanted to be a black winemaker, I never set out to be the spokesperson for AAAV either. I'm still trying to wrap my head around all of it, but I'm very honored to be in the position I'm in. The association was started by Mac McDonald in 2002 because he was recognized as a phenomenal winemaker. He was making mid 90-point Pinots from Sonoma but, when he went to events, he said people didn't look like him. He founded the AAAV and I think there were six or eight founding members. I met Mac somewhere around 2012 or 13 at a Black History Month event. Little did I know he was grooming me as his replacement. I became Vice President in 2018 and President in 2020. The interesting thing about the wine industry and diversity is we are at where we are for many reasons. When the Europeans migrated to the US, they came here with grapevines in their pockets. We didn't get here that way, so we started off behind the eight ball. If you had a bowl of jellybeans, of all the people, the colors, the creeds, the genders of people who drank wine in the world, and you looked at that bowl of jellybeans, you'd see every color imaginable. Isn't it time that the bowl of jellybeans that represent the people who make wine looked the same?

That really is the ultimate goal - trying to create diversity among the industry. We're all just humans here and I really think that's the key -- just being a good human. The goal of AAAV is to assist African American winemakers, people of color, elevate them in the industry to try to get that landscape to look like that other bowl of jellybeans.

CC: How are you using your role at AAAV to create awareness for young BIPOC people who might be just as uninformed about the wine industry as you were and let them see the wine industry as a field they can get into and have a successful career in?

PL: That's the hard part, right? Because I just didn't know it existed. There's a very narrow niche of schools that offer oenology and viticulture, some that do it very well. Cal Poly Pomona, where I went, they offer plant science and agriculture, not necessarily a viticulture and oenology program. Awareness is really important, starting with young people. That's why Longevity is trying to partner with the local college here, Las Positas, in partnering with mentorship and internship for young people. And again, a big focus of AAAV are the scholarships. When I took over, we had only awarded two scholarships in the entire existence of the organization, and in the last year, we've awarded over three dozen.

Trying to pave the path for young African American students or young students who believe in diversity is key, and that's why we focus on scholarships a lot and the awareness is a big piece of the puzzle.

CC: How do you make the need to increase awareness about African American wine not just an issue of race but, like you said, a genuinely human issue?

PL: I think part of the process, especially in light of Black Lives Matter, as a President, I really had to focus on getting out the bandwagon, because they're out there, and there are people that are going to want to jump on the bus, because that's the bus that's going the farthest right now.

In the end, the goal of AAAV is to partner with serious entities and partners who are serious about a long-term change in diversity in this industry. We have some great partners like Wine Enthusiast Magazine, like Jean-Charles Boisset, even Bronco. These are all serious partners that want to make a change.

We're going to be doing a collaborative with One Hope Winery, a few long labels that will give back to AAAV. Jean-Charles Boisset came up with a wine called Unity and half of the proceeds went to AAAV, and these are all mechanisms to use to keep the awareness going, to keep trying to push the narrative that there are African American winemakers, and we make pretty good wine. And if it's a career that you want to get into, even as a kid, hey, let us show you what we did, and that's what we try to do every day.

The takeaway

"Be a strong voice for change and provide tangible opportunities to minority communities through scholarships, partnerships and mentoring."

Conversation III

EPISODE 780 – JAMIE EVANS

The audio

The issues

This episode spotlights a different voice within the wine industry – cannabis-infused wine - and presents diversity and inclusion in a new and unusual way. Jamie's enthusiasm for what she does, and her commitment to creating an open and welcoming new arm of the hospitality sector is irresistible and this conversation is packed with information and insights. The crossover of storytelling and education mirrors the wine world and it's very interesting to think of cannabis as a partner for wine rather than a competitor.

The guest

Jamie Evans is a Certified Specialist of Wine with over a decade of wine industry experience. She's worked with the likes of Jackson Family Wines, Folio Fine Wine Partners, and Napa Valley Grape Growers. In 2017, she founded The Herb Somm, a culinary-meets-cannabis blog that's focused on the gourmet side of the cannabis industry. She's an entrepreneur, an author, and she's specializing in cannabis now, with events, tastings, CBD, cannabis food recipes, wine, essentially the whole canna-culinary world, with a new venture on her hands, Herbacée.

The conversation

CC: You were born in California, studied wine, viticulture and wine business at Cal Poly. You then travelled all over the globe studying wine. You're a Certified Specialist of Wine and a French Wine Scholar. What on earth brought you to the decision to ditch wine and move into the world of cannabis?

JE: My relationship with cannabis began back in college. I can remember coming home from my wine sensory evaluation classes at Cal Poly and smelling through all these different cannabis strains and thinking to myself, wow, these two things are so similar, the aromas and the flavors. Back then there really wasn't a lot of information about cannabis and, of course, the conversation was a lot different to what we're experiencing today. It really wasn't until January 2017 that I began using cannabis for more medical purposes. Around that time, I witnessed a terrible car accident near my home in Sausalito and it was pretty traumatic. I really couldn't sleep, and I didn't want to turn to pharmaceutical drugs. I didn't want to heavily drink alcohol, so I turned to cannabis to help me work through this trauma because it was just this more natural alternative.

As I started learning and researching about cannabis, I realized there were so many similarities between wine, which of course is my first love, and cannabis, which later became my muse! But the ways in which cannabis works with our internal systems is really what led to my career change and to what I'm doing today.

There are hundreds and hundreds of cannabis strains out there, just like wine, and just like how we develop a palate for wine tasting, you can also develop a palate for cannabis. It's all about sensory training. Like grape varieties, cannabis strains are unique. They each have their own look, their own smell, their own taste and effect, which is actually pretty interesting.

Cannabis is also terroir expressive, so it really makes it a fascinating plant to learn more about, especially coming from the wine side, where I have been focused on sensory evaluation and terroir and appellations ever since I was 18 when I started studying at Cal Poly. It really was this kind of natural bridge to think about cannabis in this way.

What I like to teach my readers and teach my guests who come to my events is, by learning to use the sensory evaluation techniques with cannabis, we can not only learn the differences between several strains, but it also helps us identify top quality flowers. It helps us identify terpene profiles, faults in cannabis, and more. By learning to discover, I call it your herbal palate, you can train yourself to really become an herb sommelier or an herb connoisseur, which really begins with this thorough understanding of terpenes. Once you're familiar with terpenes, you can really train your nose to pick out these profiles in your cannabis, just like we do with wine.

CC: Is there such a thing as cannabis education? We all know there are numerous levels of wine education.

JE: Absolutely. Out here in the U.S. there is a program developed by the Trichome Institute. It's very similar to a wine sommelier program but they call it "interpening", so you're interpreting terpenes.
During this program I work quite closely with Trichome Institute founder Max Montrose.
They've basically set up a program that teaches you the ins and outs of cannabis. You learn all about the evolution of the Global Cannabis Association, what to call thousands of cultivars, cannabis history, terminology, appellations and so on. It is very much like the wine certifications that are out there, and you can move through this program and become a certified "interpener".
CC: With wine, we swirl, we sniff, we drink it. With cannabis, how do you go about the whole tasting? Obviously, not everybody is smoking cannabis anymore. How are you ingesting it? How are you tasting it? How are you laying out the scent profile?
JE: What I love to do is put my cannabis in a wine glass and then to really evaluate the aromas. The wine glass is really the perfect vessel to do this and really smell all the different layers that are in each cannabis strain. Like what we do with wine, you could line up different cannabis strains side by side and go through and smell each different one. You'll just be so surprised that there are so many different nuances between these strains. Also, a lot of these aromas and flavors are found in wine, which is quite fascinating. For taste, what I like to do if you're smoking cannabis, what I like to recommend is using a dry flower vaporizer, which is a tool that you can find that really helps you vaporize cannabis flower so you

can actually taste that true terpene profile. At the dinners that I host this is something that I have all my guests do. They're smelling cannabis in a wine glass. They're tasting cannabis. I also like to pair cannabis with wine. This is another way of educating people on how to think about cannabis on a deeper level, really focusing on that sensory evaluation which we were talking about earlier.

CC: When you're pairing cannabis with wine, do you go for flavor and aroma profiles that match or that complement each other or that stand apart from each other. How do you do that pairing?

JE: The simplest way to approach it, especially for people who are new to cannabis, is to look for those similar tasting profiles. On my website, it's called theherbsomm.com, I actually created a terpene aroma and pairing guide, which lists the six most common terpenes found in cannabis. Then it lists all the aromas and flavors that you're looking for, in particular strains. I've also supplied some recommended food and wine pairings. This is a tool that I give to everyone at my events, so you're tasting, you're looking at this grid and piecing everything together. With these educational tools and by thinking about how these things are related. Do they taste the same? Do they smell the same? It's a really fun and interesting thing to do. Of course, you can always contrast flavors too, but I think step one is teaching people how to find kind of those similar aromas and flavors.

CC: You started Thursday Infused in 2018, which is a gourmet event series that highlights all the different cannabis chefs across the US. What's the focus? What's

the objective of the series? How do you perceive the "cannabis meets culinary" world? How is the crossover between cannabis and fine dining or modern cuisine going to develop in the future, in your opinion?
JE: Cannabis is such an amazing ingredient to cook with. Not only does it add unique aromas and flavors to the meal, but it adds this sense of euphoria. When I started my Thursday Infused event series, it was really this idea of working with different cannabis chefs across the U.S. to bring this pairing concept to life, but also teach people how to consume cannabis infused foods safely and responsibly and really showcase cannabis as a gourmet ingredient. At my events, from start to finish, I really like to take my guests on this sensory journey, highlighting the complexities and similarities between wine, food and cannabis. You're really pairing three things together at these meals, and there's an art to crafting the experience. These are low dose dinners as well, because the food is infused.
The most important thing to gauge when you're hosting an infused dinner is the comfort level of your guests. I would check in with each guest that was coming to the dinner and ask them, what level of THC [Tetrahydrocannabinol] are you comfortable consuming? When you're approaching cannabis, it's really important to remember that it's such an individualized medicine. Everybody is so different with how they can consume.
The chefs at these dinners are so amazing too, because they can precisely dose each guest meal based on those preferences. I had some guests come, they're maybe just comfortable with 2.5 milligrams of THC throughout

the entire meal. We can certainly accommodate that. Or I have some guests who prefer a higher dose because they are used to eating infused foods, they're comfortable at a higher level, and we can accommodate that too.We usually create these four-course tasting dinners. I sit down with the chef, I sit down with our cannabis farmer, I've had lots of farmers come down for these events, and I usually sit down with a wine partner. Before the event, we taste the cannabis, we taste the wine, we have the chef there, and we're really thinking about what flavors are working together, what ingredients we want to highlight through this meal. We put the menu together. It's very thoughtful.

Usually, we also like to incorporate some different cannabinoids throughout the meal. Of course, we're going to have some THC, but we usually like to do THC at the beginning of the meal and then incorporate some non-intoxicating cannabinoids, maybe some CBD [Cannabidiol], some THCA [Tetrahydrocannabinolic acid] throughout the other courses to really help ground out that experience. It's really about taking your guests on this journey and educating along the way because I firmly believe that education is so important, especially when it comes to cannabis.

I am recalling one of my events. I worked with this amazing chef. Her name is chef Haijun Chen of Big Bad Wolf. And during one of the meals, she made this gorgeous salmon sashimi and topped it with a citrus sauce. With that course, we paired it with a rosé that expressed a similar citrus profile that also matched perfectly well with the salmon's sweeter notes. The flower that we chose was called Tangi, which is rich in the terpene called limonene, which really gives those citrus notes as well. When you're pairing all of these things together, they have the similarity of the citrus profile and on your palate, everything is just working together as a great wine and food pairing would.

CC: You bring your cannabis farmers in, and you're donating part of your event revenues to local non-profits in the San Francisco Bay Area that are creating sustainable urban farms and gardens. I'm assuming some of these will be cannabis farmers as well. How are you collaborating with these farmers and these gardeners?

JE: With the cannabis farmers, I always like to showcase cannabis flower throughout the meal, but I also think it's so important for the cannabis farmer to get face time with the consumer, and it's just so amazing.

CC: You don't normally think about your cannabis producer in the same way that you think about your Chianti producer!

JE: Exactly. Every time I've had them at my dinners, they're just so passionate about the plant, they're passionate about their flower, and they can paint the picture of where the cannabis came from, the soil the cannabis was grown in, and the steps of creating this beautiful product. To hear the story from the farmer is so important for consumers to know that story.

Much like wine, we want to know where our wine comes from, we want to know who grows the wine, who produces the wine, and so on. I think that's a large part of cannabis, which maybe we don't talk about as often as we should. Supporting these farmers has always been a very critical part of what I do. We donate a portion of event sales revenue to our farmers.

I was working with an organization called City Slicker Farms here in the Bay Area, and they're dedicated to building these high yield urban farms and backyard gardens for the community. It's really important to me to give back to our community, which, coming from cannabis, this is such a critical part of supporting the community. That's where those relationships started. Once I bring my event series back, I would love to continue to support their mission.

I've actually helped, I participated in one of their urban garden builds as well. It was just really fun to get out there and help with the initiative.

Luckily, I'm based here in the San Francisco Bay Area, and this area is bustling with cannabis chefs, edible producers. Before COVID, there was a lot of cannabis focused events and beyond. What I've learned has been a lot of personal research, but also from these amazing people in the industry. Because of this supportive community, I've really learned the ins and outs of the culinary cannabis world.

Even when I was hosting my Thursday Infused event, I would learn something each time from each of these cannabis chefs and their approach to cooking with cannabis. The culinary side, too, is just so incredibly fascinating, and we're just at the beginning of cooking with cannabis. A lot of what I've learned is from these amazing people I've interviewed and that I work with and also a lot of personal research. Once people understand and learn the process of cooking with cannabis, it just opens the door to so many new experiences.

I firmly believe that education is the key to breaking the stigma that surrounds cannabis. Since launching The Herb Somm, I've been really focused on building out this educational platform to educate consumers on how to incorporate cannabis into daily life, but in a very safe and responsible manner. As we talked about earlier, by curating and hosting interactive dining experiences, I've also found that cannabis is more approachable and relatable when combined with food and beverages.

When we frame it that way and talk about cannabis with food and beverages, it makes people feel more comfortable. They're more open to asking questions, especially when they're coming to these infused meals. They're with their friends, they're laughing, it's a very inviting environment. I feel like the food and beverage side of cannabis is also bringing in more curious consumers because we live in a society that loves food and beverages. It's a really great way to frame education around those things.

CC: I love your packaging, it's absolutely beautiful and you're using bottles and cans. It's a sparkling rosé, so a south of France inspired blend made with Grenache, in these really gorgeous looking, floral covered bottles and cans, what's the marketing strategy?

JE: The inspiration behind Herbacée flowers that's on all our packaging really came from the desire to celebrate Mother Nature's bounty. This includes plants, flowers, of course, cannabis, and all the different herbs that really provide us with so many different healing properties. As a non-alcoholic cannabis-infused wine,

Herbacée means herbaceous in French, which is a term that we use in the wine industry to describe herbal notes in wine.

This product really explores this divine connection between cannabis and the grapevine because both plants are terpene rich, they offer this wide array of botanical aromas and flavors, we really wanted to bring this concept to life through our packaging, through our messaging.

If you look at our bottles and cans, they're very floral, and it makes you feel like you're in a flower field drinking rosé. We have the cans available right now, and then hopefully our 750s will be bottled this year. That is the vision, and I would love to start building out our sparkling wine cannabis wine portfolio. We have our sparkling rosé, which is actually called sparkling rosea because of the California regulations, but we're also launching a sparkling blanc this spring, which I'm calling sparkling blanchette.

In the cannabis space itself, there's really only a handful of cannabis infused wine brands at this moment, only five or six in total, which isn't a lot. From the cannabis beverage side, I really consider us more collaborators than competitors at this point, because it is such a young category and we're all learning together along the way.

The non-alcoholic category is where we fall into, but also it is a great alternative to alcohol. For those people who are looking to cut back or just not drink alcohol at all, cannabis beverages are a perfect alternative to explore.

This is one of the most exciting parts. In one can, which is 10oz per can, there's only ten calories.

It's pretty incredible. That's because of the dealcoholizing process and something about this specific brand, as well. I really wanted to create a dry style wine, I don't want to add a ton of extra sugar, which is sometimes something that we find in a lot of non-alcoholic wines in general, is it's coated with sugar. I really wanted to have this dry beverage with bright acidity that pairs well with food. I've tried so many different pairings so far with our sparkling rosea and I just love the bright acidity profile.

The takeaway

"Stimulate the market and reinvent the appeal of traditional wine products through innovation, while encouraging new discussions of wine's place alongside emerging products."

Conversation IV

EPISODE 755 – NTSIKI BAYELLA

The audio

The issues

Becoming the first black female winemaker in South Africa was a journey I just had to explore with Ntsiki and her story is utterly inspiring.

The guest

Ntsiki Biyela is the award-winning winemaker and director of Aslina Wines, a company named in honor of her late grandmother. Biyela was awarded a scholarship through South African Airways to study winemaking at the University of Stellenbosch in 1999. She graduated in 2003 with a BSc in Agriculture (Viticulture and Oenology) and joined Stellekaya, a boutique winery, as their winemaker in 2004. In 2009, she was crowned Woman Winemaker of the Year. In 2017, she was named in the Top 20 Most Innovative Women in Food and Drinks by Fortune Magazine. She has also been named one of the top 15 Women in Wine to Watch by Food and Wine Magazine in the USA.

The conversation

CC: You had never tasted wine before you were offered a scholarship to study wine making at Stellenbosch University. What made you decide to accept that scholarship and go into winemaking?

NB: It wasn't really winemaking *per se* that made me take the scholarship. It was a need to change my life. It was a need to do something. When the scholarship came and they said, why me? I said, I'll take it because I wanted to change my life. I wanted to study. Those are the key things that I wanted. The fact that it came in winemaking, it wasn't really the reason for choosing it, but the reason was to change my life.

CC: What were you doing before the scholarship came along?

NB: I finished matriculation [high school] and I started applying for bursaries [to university]. But all the bursaries I was applying for, I was getting the very famous letters coming back saying we regret… So, I got a job, I worked for a year as a domestic worker. When I got called at school, I was already working as a domestic worker. I worked for a year, and then I got this opportunity to apply for this scholarship, which I did in 1998. I was working and then I got the scholarship to Stellenbosch. It wasn't really about wine. It was learning in Afrikaans. That was a tricky part, it was learning in a different culture. It was being in a different environment, which doesn't look like the environment I grew up in, which doesn't feel like the environment I grew up in, culturally and in all aspects of it. It was basically more challenging. For me it was one of those times to say, no matter what comes my way, I need to get this degree, I need to pass, I need to succeed in what I'm doing.

CC: Going into Stellenbosch, were there other black students in your class?

NB: There were in our class probably a handful. In our class we were a handful of black people, but the rest were obviously white students. One of the things that was making it even more difficult was the language barrier, because we don't understand the language, it was making it tricky. It was really hard.

I guess when you say the word that I used, "tricky," is really very light for what it was, I guess it was probably just a choice of words. But as I think about our studies, there were moments of tears, there were moments of crying. One thing I'm grateful for is that not even once did I have a thought of saying I'm going to throw in the towel. There was another battle. When it comes to students, the lecturer will try to speak English in class, trying to accommodate us who didn't understand Afrikaans, and the white students will make noise and say, it's an Afrikaans University, you're not going to do that. So, there was that. It was very interesting that in our final year, only in our final year, really that we started bonding, but it was right at the end. During the process, where for a couple of years, it was really hard. Even if the lecturer would want to assist, so much so that we ended up having to have extra classes. You go to class and then you ask for extra classes and where to get tutors. The lecturers will appoint a master's student or a PhD student to be a tutor so that we've got a second class after class. We had to do everything twice with very little support.

I think it's only now as an adult that I'm realizing the importance of the strength of my foundation. I had my grandmother when she was alive. She was one person, I knew that when I go home, I'm fetching my strength to go and fight the battle, because when you came to a corner, you realize being outside of home or outside of campaign, that's a battlefield. Going home, I'll come back. My grandmother is very spiritual. I'll get home, and then when I leave and she'll pray, and then I'll feel like, you know what? I can do anything now. And then I'll go back to university and start back up. Also knowing that I got sisters, I have a family and then friends. Those were the people, the community that you need as a person to go crying to. When the situation gets tough, people are going to say, we know it's hard, but we know you can do it, it's hard, but we are here. They might not be there for your books, but they are there. You know they are there. I used to call one of my sisters who was based in Derby, and I called her crying. I remember the first time I called, I said I dreamed I had failed and the university kicked me out and I was crying. She was like, no, it was a dream because you were stressing. I couldn't say that I was just so afraid of failing. That drove me to find out what other opportunities or other help that is there. I found out that there was student counselling on campus. I had to attend that, go to counselling and say, look, I've got issues here. This is a battle. This is a struggle. I'm going to fail. To explain everything, that I'm going to be kicked out, but I can't go back home because I'm going back to nothing. I need to make it work here. You guys are going to help me make it work.

I think it's one of those things that knowing and understanding that if I go back to nothing, then what? I have to make it work. As I'm saying, it looks like you feel like everything has to be. And I'm like, yes, it has to be, but you need to be gentle with it. No, I have to pass. The counsellor couldn't understand my situation and I don't understand why you're so adamant that it must be like that. That was it. Until they had said, okay, fine if you fail, because you are attending therapy, we will write a letter, the university will not kick you out. And then that basically gave me a good safety net. Now I can put all my energy to try to figure out this thing. Luckily, I passed that year.

CC: How did you get from university to Stellekaya?

NB: I had applied because when I was a student because I was working part time for one of the wineries. I worked for Delheim Wines, working in the vineyard, working basically everywhere, because I needed to understand the crop that I'm doing, because I had no idea. I had no idea of wine.

That is where I learned about wine as a student. When I finished my studies, I started applying for jobs. Looking for a wine-making job or a cultural job. Luckily, when I applied at Stellekaya they called me for an interview and then they hired me. They saw what they wanted. It happened to be the kind of place I was looking for myself, because I knew when I was studying that when I go out to work, I want to work in a small company so that I can learn about all the aspects of the business, because at some point I want to start my own business. I was clear.

Stellekaya was a small company, still small, but we were just starting. I had a consultant who was a previous winemaker, and the accounts lady was the one basically holding my hand to say, okay, fine, you need to order bottles, this is where you're going to get your bottles, just to give me direction.

And the cellar supervisor was the one who was holding my hand in the cellar to say, okay, we've got barrels here, we've got this there, just to get that. Getting in the door with a lesson that my mother taught me. She said to me, know that as you go to that company, that everyone you find in there, they know better than you because they've been with the company. Everyone in that company is going to teach you. It does not matter whether you're going to come in as their supervisor, their manager, or whatever. But the bottom line is they know better than you.

A colleague's wife was working in the kitchen, and she used to treat me like one of her kids. I was always running around, and she would come with coffee and a toasted sandwich. She'd literally get in there with a cup and put the sandwich on the table and close the door and stop and say, you're going to sit and eat, and I'll be like, but I need to work. She would make me sit and eat. Then I'd just sit down and eat. It was more like it was family. It was like having family at work.

CC: You were named the first black female winemaker in South Africa in 2004 and then you won a gold medal for your first red wine.

NB: Yes, that was a Cape Cross, it was a Cape blend, Pinotage, Cabernet Sauvignon and Merlot. It was the International Wine Awards, when the awards were announced, it was very interesting that in the room at the event, I remember clearly, there were two black people. It was me and a winemaker from Zimbabwe. It was the two of us as black people, and then the rest of the black people were the waiters and waitresses. What touched me most that evening is when the awards were being announced, and when they called Stellekaya Cape Cross, the waiters and waitresses screamed with excitement. I was like, oh my God, they know me. It was a moving moment. It was that moment of coming in, thinking we have only two people here, two black people in this whole room that's full of people in the industry. To actually say, no, we're not only two, at the same time, they [the wait staff] are all part of this. It was really nice.

CC: In 2009, you were named South Africa's Woman Winemaker of the Year.

NB: The award was based on submitting the wine tasted blind. My wine was a 2006 Cabernet Sauvignon, that got me that award. Yeah, it was exciting. Very exciting. We were looking at that. We were reflecting on that last year, because when I got that award, and it was a milestone at that moment. The people that were giving the award were part of the Michelangelo International Wine & Spirits Award. Last year, when our wine Umsasane got a trophy at Michelangelo, it was like, oh, my goodness, we have come full circle the whole way.

CC: Well, I'm curious, though, the title you won with South Africa's Woman Winemaker of the Year, would you rather just be Winemaker of the Year? What do you think about the woman distinction?

NB: Well, I feel everything's got its space. There was

a woman winemaker competition. It ran its course. In general, obviously, as wine makers, we're all winemakers, whether you're a woman or not. We're all wine makers. We all started the same thing, all basically peddling on the same path. The only difference, as women, we know that it's been a journey. So, as women we're trying to find a place in space and trying to find a way. So that's why that award probably was created, to find a way in the space. It ran well…

CC: You've always said you see the potential of black South Africans as wine consumers because white winemakers weren't tapping into that. This clearly is something you've been working on for a long time, breaking down these barriers.

NB: Yes. When someone presents something to you, it's different. Don't present it from their own perspective, don't present something to you from their own understanding. But how much more when someone is presenting something to you in their own perspective and you find out that actually I relate because that's where I'm from and that's where I am. It's just that way of understanding.

For me, when it comes to the wine industry, talking about wine, talking about food, is that when we talk about food and food parents, we still talk about the Western culture. As black people, the food we eat, our own real food, well some people now eat the pastas, they have steaks and stuff, but we eat dumplings. We eat tripe. There are certain foods that are our foundation, that we grew up eating, that we like eating. An example for me, I cannot go for a long time without having pap [maize porridge]. I feel like I'm getting weak, so I have to have it.

For now, especially when I do wine tastings and talking to people about their flavors or the characteristics that I'm picking up in the wine, I try to talk about characteristics that I grew up with, talking about things that we're eating and things that people don't have to go out there and go look for, things that are written on the back labels. But look at what you have in your fridge. Cook the food that you normally cook and see if it works.

Just an example, I remember at some point when I was working at Stellekaya, I tasted Merlot. Now, I love making chicken curry, I use masala because my grandmother used to, I'll make my dumplings, could be chicken dumplings, but I use masala curry powder. I had this masala chicken curry, and I tasted it with Merlot. One of the things that people say, red wine and curry run for your life, right? And then I made that. I remember it was at night, I called my colleague at night and I'm like, you won't believe what just happened, I'm having Merlot and chicken curry and it's the bomb! It's amazing! Till today, that is one pairing that it happened, just not because I thought I'm going to pair this. I was like, I'm cooking, I feel like eating this, and I'm going to make myself chicken curry and a bottle of wine, and that's what I did.

CC: You started your own winery in 2017 and the name of the winery is Aslina.

NB: Yes. I named the company after my grandmother, in honor of her because she played a big role, and I still feel she's playing a big role in my life and in today's spiritual me. For me, it was important to pay tribute to the great person in my life.

I like the fact that in South Africa, unlike probably in France, you can have a wine company without having a winery, without having a vineyard or anything. The way of starting was basically to rent a cellar space from those who have got cellars, buy grapes from those who are convenient and make the wine. Most winemakers who started their own brand, that's what they do. It's a common practice in South Africa.

Working at Stellekaya gave me all that experience and helped me to build those relationships with cellars and growers, so when I finished, it wasn't a matter of starting from scratch. It was a matter of going to the people I know. Do you have any extra grapes? I want this out like that, block up like this. It's basically going on through the people that I've been working with before and building new relationships and getting new suppliers of grapes.

CC: Well, you've been working pretty much non-stop for the past 20 years. But you've still found time to be a board member for Pinotage Youth Development Academy.

NB: At the Academy, basically, we are training young people through the value chain of the wine industry. These are the 18- to 25-year-olds. They get to the Academy, get trained, and receive placement within the industry and the hospitality. We're trying to expand that. For me, as well as being the board member, what I like the most is I see myself in the students and I see the growth. It's always exciting when I see them, when they're starting at the beginning of the year, when they start, and then you see the person at the end how they have grown and how they've changed and how they've developed because they already have the talent.

It's just they need that extra step just to help them understand themselves and become the best people they are.

CC: In 2017, Forbes magazine named you one of the top 20 most innovative women in food and drinks. Where are you going to go from here?

NB: Well, I think now that we've got the Chenin Blanc that I've always wanted or this very skin contact white wine that I've always wanted, one of the things we're trying to work on now is to get our own facility. Other than renting, our growth is now based on our growing to be able to get our own facility

CC: And do you have dreams of your own vineyard?

NB: Absolutely. I'm excited about this. It's one step at a time.

The takeaway

"Understand the significant barriers that continue to exist in sectors of the wine world, build strategies to surmount them; recognize the diverse range of cultural reference points held by consumers and producers alike."

Conversation V

EPISODE 743 – DR HOBY WEDLER

The audio

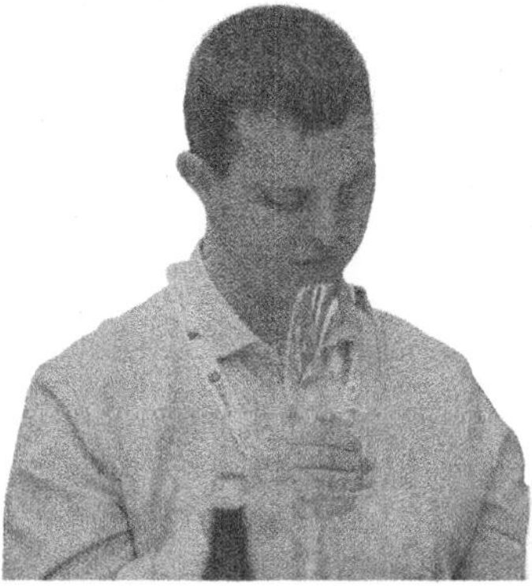

The issues

I chose this episode to explore another aspect of exclusion in the wine industry and how one brilliant, humble man can make a startling impact on the way we think and talk about wine.

The guest

Dr. Hoby Wedler has a PhD in organic chemistry from the University of California, Davis and is the founder and owner of Tasting in the Dark. In 2021 he was named one of Wine Enthusiasts 40 under 40 Tastemakers.

The conversation

CC: Let's address the big issue right here first of all, you've been blind from birth.

HW: Absolutely, totally blind since birth. I like to say that, yes, I am totally blind, and I wouldn't want it any other way. I've learned how to live my life as a blind person and I know the world around me, and I love the world around me, so that's what I appreciate. If I got my sight back, I'd have to relearn things. So, I'm a proud blind man, let's just say that.

CC: Where did you find the inspiration and the wherewithal to become, of all things, a chemist? It sounds dangerous.

HW: That's funny. That's a great question. I've always had a deep fascination for really how things work and how things fit together. I remember vividly standing in my parents' kitchen in April 1991 when I was just about four years old and turning on the tap to get a glass of water. I had done this hundreds of times, but it dawned on me that water was actually flowing out of this faucet into my glass. Where the heck was this water coming from? That led to a whole fascination of, wow, there's plumbing throughout a city that brings water to everyone's home. Where are these pipes running? How do they work? That led to a trip to the water resources department and all sorts of things.

My parents were just so excited about me exploring the world around me and I remember another example a few years later of plugging in the vacuum cleaner and turning it on and having it hum to life. I was going to clean my room and I thought what the heck is running this thing? How are electrons flowing? I know that we don't pay for electrons, do we? That led to a whole discussion of electricity with my father and understanding that really what we don't pay for the electrons themselves, those are fairly recycled, rather, we pay for the electromotive force or voltage that pushes those electrons through a wire.

One thing led to another, and I think a lot of people have passions that are developed, grown up from childhood, but really developed by excellent teachers. I had a wonderful high school physical science teacher who ended up being my chemistry teacher. With her I just fell in love with chemistry. I was so passionate about it, it was what drove me to enjoy science. When it came time to take a test to see if I would get into honors chemistry, of course, I tried and scored high on that test, and she couldn't really deny me the opportunity to sit in that class, but we had to figure out how we would make it accessible.

We did very well. We brought a student in, one year my senior, who worked as my eyes in the laboratory and scribed my answers on tests, but I did everything else. It was interesting because in many ways, this instructor would tell the class, "Chemistry. You might think of it as just a prerequisite to do what you think you want to do, but really, it's the study of how things work. It's what we eat, it's what we drink, it's what we breathe. Chemistry is everything. You all should think about studying chemistry at a more thorough level than just what you need it for in college." I don't think the rest of the class was particularly interested. I was different. I loved chemistry and thought, oh yeah, this is exciting, I want to study chemistry for my career because I want to teach it and inspire others, as I was inspired. I would talk to her alone and say, I really want to study chemistry. How do you think I should do this as a blind person? She would say, "Well, I don't think this makes sense for you. I think it's not necessarily the right direction for you to go, blah, blah, blah." I said, okay this is interesting. Now I got to think about why I think chemistry and a career in chemistry makes sense to me. I remember vividly the second week of the second semester of my high school career with her, my junior year, I went into her classroom, and I said I understand that you think chemistry is a visual science, but I have to tell you that nobody can see atoms.

Chemistry is really a cerebral science, where we use our vision or our eyesight, rather, to understand a few things that might happen in the laboratory, but really chemistry is something that we think about and ponder in our mind. She said, "wow, that's really interesting. I appreciate you for that". She became a great supporter and a true ally and still is a dear friend and ally. She encouraged me then to go on to UC Davis and study chemistry as an undergraduate. That led to me wanting to teach chemistry at the college level and apply for my PhD. I found a great chemistry mentor and I did that. I had the honor of teaching some general chemistry classes, which is what I wanted to teach as a graduate student, and I realized that students didn't necessarily like to read the textbook and they didn't speak chemistry. They wanted to see a bunch of photos and videos and cute animations and this sort of thing. I was like, why am I spending a lot of time and money, frankly, working with assistants, making these beautiful presentations, and then spending a lot of time trying to memorize these presentations so I could present them coherently, because they were not accessible to me, they were accessible to my students. I thought, why am I spending all this time trying to make something accessible to my students when it's hard to make accessible to me without assistance? That's what led me into entrepreneurship. It's actually how, in graduate school, I got into wine.

CC: So, you decided to become an entrepreneur instead of staying in the classroom. How did that go?

HW: First of all, in general, I got excited about entrepreneurship at the end of my graduate tenure, because I realized that it was for me. For 95 plus percent of entrepreneurs, entrepreneurship is not about money or power, right? Rather, it's really about solving problems and creating a business entity to solve an important problem. What I realized is that I've been doing this since day one for my survival as a blind person in a sighted world. I had a really good diverse approach. Could I solve problems for people that they didn't even know they needed solutions to? That's what really led me into wanting to be an entrepreneur.

The way that I got into wine is kind of a fun story. Right at the very end of my undergraduate tenure, in the beginning of my graduate work in 2011, a mutual friend introduced me to Francis Ford Coppola. Coppola's team called me and said, hey what do you think of hosting a tasting with Francis, a truly blindfolded wine experience? When Francis team says jump, you say okay, what are we doing here? Let's do it. When they call and ask you to do something, you say yes. Then I hung up and said, oh my God, what did I just agree to do?

I worked with Francis to develop a wine experience, and it was really my own wine experience that he approved. The innovation was between me and a lot of his amazing winemakers and team at the winery. The goal was to create a truly blindfolded wine experience. It was a lot of fun to build and create that. To me it was not about using the blindfold as a game or a gimmick, but rather about creating an opportunity to think about wine in a few different ways, when we're not distracted by our eyesight. We use eyesight to obtain 85% to 90% of the information from our surroundings, which is interesting because it's one out of five senses that we use for so much information mining, which means to me that we have four additional perfectly good senses which we only use to take in 10% to 15% of the world around us.

My whole theory is, come on, let's drive forward and see what we can do with our other senses. It's been a great experience working with sighted people to show them how they can experience something, whether it's a conversation that we have while we're getting ready to taste or the actual wine itself, I think they find it really rewarding.

As soon as it was picked up by the Francis Ford Coppola national sales team, I got to travel a lot throughout the years of 2013, 2014, etc. What was great about my chemistry is that I studied computational chemistry in graduate school because being in the lab wasn't all that safe for me without an assistant. My laptop was my laboratory, and I had an incredible graduate chemistry advisor who said, you need to explore the world around you, there are limitless opportunities and maybe you don't want to study chemistry for your whole career, so get out there and go forth and conquer. For me, that was really exciting to hear, it was a great opportunity.

I said, okay, let me do this. I travelled with Coppola's team a lot. That was when I met a lot of people and discovered the world of food and beverage, and, in particular, the world of wine. By the way, this tasting in the dark experience has branched out into many markets and food and beverage and other industries throughout the world. It was when I realized that wine people and food people are my kind of people as well. Maybe this is a space that I really wanted to work and grow and offer my palate, which I didn't realize I'd trained to be a strong palate until I started hosting people and realizing that for my whole life, I've been remembering aromas almost as vocabulary. It spawned that way. We all have our ups and downs in our entrepreneurial journey. Mine's been five years, it's just burgeoning, but I've already had some great ups and great downs, and we just keep moving forward and figuring out what makes the most sense.

Tasting in the Dark is one of the things that I do as a speaker. I also have a company where I consult on product development in and outside of wine, but mostly in food and drink. I do a lot of experience design, which is great fun as well, designing high end experiences that take advantage of not only the sense of eyesight, but all our senses, sometimes while depriving the sense of sight. Tasting in the Dark, particularly as it pertains to wine, is an experience where guests, I've done it for, as few as one and as many as 400, sit around tables, oftentimes we'll blindfold them before bringing them into the room where they'll be tasting, then we walk them into the room and show them where their seat is. We take time to let them feel what's on the table in front of them, or we'll walk them in sighted and then have them put their blindfolds on and not pour anything until the blindfold is on. The point is for them not to be aware of the color or shape or anything visually of what's in the cups in front of them.

We start out by having a conversation about wine. How is wine an art? How is wine an art form just as profound as painting or sculpture or drawing or photography or music or screenplays or anything? Wine, and food and drink in general, really are art forms that have to be considered. We also talk about how wine really straddles the intersection so beautifully of art and science.

There's a very narrow line between these two fields. I like to tell people that, simply put, science is really, if we think about it, like building a house. Science is the tools that we need. It's the lumber, it's the screws, it's the hammers, it's the drills, it's everything we need, the foundation. It's everything we need to physically build the house. Art is how we build it, what we put where, how we design it. This sort of thing is all art. We talk about how wine is just this beautiful sort of amalgamation, if you will, of science and art.

Then we talk about the whole, we don't need to use our eyesight for so much of what we take in from our surroundings, and you really don't need to see to love life. We make wine subjective. We say, you know what kind of art you like, but if you don't taste enough wine, you won't know what kind of wine you like, and it's okay, even if they're a very high-quality wine, for me to like something and you not to like it, and vice versa. I like to prime people's palates by calibrating their aromatic vocabulary, so I bring in anywhere from two to six different aroma samples that I pick out of the wines that people are tasting and hand design myself, whether it's citrus or stone fruit or anise or oak or tobacco or whatever the case may be.

We smell those and we talk about those calibrated aromas.

Then we sit around the table and together we taste four to six wines and have a really wonderful conversation and wonderful time together, tasting wine and talking about wine and appreciating each other. It's an amazing opportunity for everyone and people find it to be really engaging and stimulating of all their senses.

CC: You've recently done a project with the Solomon R. Guggenheim Foundation and Ornellaia from Tuscany.

HW: Ornellaia is one of my favorite wineries in Italy. I just need to confess, first of all, that I absolutely love Italy. I love the people, I love the culture, perhaps most importantly, I love the food and the wine of Italy. Italian wine is eminently complex and just works so well with the foods of Italy and with the culture. I love everything about Italy truthfully, especially as it pertains to great people and great food and great wine. We have to do something there sometime.

CC: How did this come about with Ornellaia and the Solomon R. Guggenheim Foundation?

HW: Ornellaia has a really special program where every year an artist comes in and does a featured sculpture, if you will. They're very iconic. They do a sculpture. They basically define that vintage by a word and do a sculpture around that word. In 2006 the word was happiness, and happily ever after is what they created in hedges around a circular bench. The print letters are done up with hedges. Just to give you an example, it's about, I'd say, four or five meters across diametrically across this circle, and it's just an absolutely gorgeous art piece. Then the artist also does a two-dimensional version which they paint on large format bottles of Ornellaia wine from that year. Those bottles are auctioned off at Sotheby's auction house.

Several years ago, Ornellaia got connected with the Solomon R. Guggenheim Museum and used the Guggenheim Foundation, not only the Museum in New York, but all five museums around the world and used the funds, the proceeds from these large format bottles to fund a program called Mind's Eye. Mind's Eye is a really amazing program because it's an opportunity for blind people or people experiencing sight loss to explore the world around them in a way that maybe they haven't ever been able to, by hearing descriptions of the artwork. It started in New York, but now it's expanded to all the Guggenheim properties, all the Guggenheim museums. Literally, art is described by docents who really practice and become excellent at describing art in words that are nonvisual. Maybe they'll bring some tactile pieces with them, maybe they'll describe it in terms of smell or feeling or emotion. Walking through, I got to do this prior to the experience that I hosted, walking through and experiencing artwork as it's described to you is really quite incredible.

In June of 2019 we did an experience, a Tasting in the

Dark experience where I hosted alongside Axel Heinz, who's the senior wine educator and wine maker for Ornellaia, in New York in the restaurant at the Guggenheim Museum on New York's Upper West Side. It was just an incredible opportunity to bring in several people from the media and publicists around the world and show them this opportunity and this experience. We actually did a little Mind's Eye tour for them. Just another aside about Mind's Eye that I think is incredible, related to the pandemic and what we just went through. As you might know, in the Guggenheim Museum, art is not allowed to be photographed at all. There are no photos, nobody could go through and photograph the museum and create a photo tour of any of the Guggenheim properties, but what they could do is describe the art in podcast form, so viewers around the world were able to get access. Sighted people and blind people alike were able to get access to the artwork of the Guggenheim during the pandemic through audio description. It's incredible to think about how one opportunity like that can lead to so many other doors swinging open and allow this torrent of opportunity for sighted folks to experience artwork in the same way.

Just to share one quick comment with you about why I love wine and romanticize wine so much. Simply put, wine for me is a way that I can taste the complexities of art. When people talk about what they can see and what landscapes look like, and then when I taste a wine, I get that same level. I don't know if it's the same experience, but it's definitely a similar level of complexity that's just absolutely gorgeous. It really paints a picture in my mind.

CC: President Obama recognized you by naming you a Champion of Change for enhancing employment and education opportunities for people with disabilities. Are you still working in that arena?

HW: I help wherever I can, so that work was just an incredible opportunity and such a humbling honor to receive that from President Obama. I received that because I founded an organization called Accessible Science, which is a non-profit aimed at hosting annual chemistry camps for blind and visually impaired high school and young college students, to show them how to do hands on chemistry. That was the hello, come do some chemistry with us and learn from chemistry professors how their work could be made accessible to you. The truth of the experience was so much deeper than that. It was really a matter of bringing people together to say, hey, what is possible when you can't see? What we try to show them is that anything is possible, and they should pursue whatever they want, no matter how visual it might seem. The world is their oyster. We had a lot of great students that we worked with, a lot of whom have gone on to receive master's degrees and PhDs and things that maybe they didn't think they could study beforehand. It was just really inspirational to do that.

I must admit that that project is going to be picked up by someone else, but it went on hiatus in 2016 when I completed my graduate work because I really needed to focus on my businesses and what I was working on. That said, whenever anybody reaches out and needs help figuring out how to access the world, how to make things more accessible, I work hard and will always accommodate that and help them personally in any way that I can, because I believe it's so important. I don't think of it as a duty, I think of it as a passion. If I was able to do some things in this world in science, maybe I can help others who have similar situations do similar things. It's a goal of mine to help everybody be whatever they can possibly be as they move forward and as they grow. That's what my work is there.

A key focal point of all of my work is making teams and making everything I do as diverse and as inclusive as possible. As we know, this is a hot topic, formed in 2020 with a series of events that we really start thinking about how we include more people and how we create a more inclusive and foster a more diverse environment in the workplace. Simply put, I feel like diversity is really such an important thing to have on a team, because if you bring more diverse skill sets to the team and more diverse minds to the table to solve problems, you're going to get a more diverse and usually more appropriate solution.

Diversity increases bottom line for a lot of companies and, if it's viewed as a positive like that, instead of, oh I have to make my team more diverse, it's so much more powerful. That's the way that I think it should be viewed by everybody. It's a really important topic to consider that when we hire for diversity, we're not hiring the diversity officer who says, okay I'm in charge of diversity and now we can check the box. Really, hiring a diverse team is organic and it involves every team member you bring on and involves serious consideration.

The takeaway

“Physical disability should not exclude anyone from wine. Teams with greater diversity are more effective and can positively impact the bottom line.”

Conversation VI

EPISODE 719 - YANNICK BENJAMIN

The audio

The issues

This was my first podcast as the host of VOICES and Yannick, who I knew previously, graciously agreed to come onboard as my first guest. I never expected the result would be a conversation that covered all my points of interest in the arena of diversity, equity and inclusion, with such insight and humanity.

The guest

Benjamin, a New York City-based sommelier, is the co-founder of Contento in East Harlem, which opened in 2021. He is also a co-founder and director of development for Wine on Wheels, an organization that helps recently disabled people. In 2003, a car accident left Benjamin paralyzed, but he pursued his dreams to attend college and become a sommelier. Having worked in his early years at Le Cirque, Jean-Georges, Felidia and Atelier at the Ritz Carlton, Benjamin went back to wine service at Le Dû's Wines for more than seven years and also became an accomplished athlete. He was named one of Wine Enthusiast's Top 40 Under 40 in 2016 and Sommelier/Beverage Director of the Year in 2021. [Food & Wine subsequently named him one of their Game Changers in 2022, after this interview took place.] Benjamin and partners opened Contento with the ethos and tagline "accessible for all". It is a stunning example of quality hospitality designed with a broadly inclusive approach.

The conversation

CC: First of all, I wanted to congratulate you on your 2021 award from Wine Enthusiast. Were you shocked or did you have an idea this was coming?

YB: No, I was certainly very shocked and honored and all of the above. It had announced the nominees along with some really fabulous professionals and friends that I highly respect. Just being nominated was such an honor. The most important thing is that this gives me a platform and I get some validation for all the work that I've done, all the good things, all the struggles, that were really a building block to where I'm at now. I really want to take advantage of that and share that platform with other people with disabilities, with other people from marginalized communities and help them get their foot in the door to what I think is a wonderful industry, both the wine and the hospitality industry. We still have a long way to go when it comes to inclusivity, and that's what I really want to do with that platform.

CC: In June 2021, you opened your first restaurant in East Harlem called Contento. I love the name. Can you explain the meaning of it to everybody and why you chose that name?

YB: When I was thinking of names for the restaurant, I really wanted names that exude positivity, names that would be memorable and easy to pronounce for all people. I was doing Google searches, I was on Google translate and I picked a word that would best describe myself and my philosophy, and that was the word happy. Happy translated to "contento", which means happy in Spanish and Italian.

It was such a perfect name for East Harlem because it was predominantly Italian immigrants in the late 1800s up until the 1940/50s, when it transitioned into mostly Central and South American and Puerto Rican. It's known now as El Barrio. I really wanted to pay homage to all of these really important personalities, to these immigrant groups, because East Harlem is what it is today because of them. This is a way to thank them for it.

CC: Contento is no ordinary restaurant. The guiding focus for the development was to create a restaurant that's barrier free and accessible to everyone, guests and employees included. What does barrier free mean for a restaurant?

YB: When I was in a car accident in 2003, I was 25 years old and prior to that, I had always worked in restaurants. My family is in the industry and by the age of 13 I had made a firm decision that this is what I wanted to do, I wanted to be in the hospitality industry. Then I had this car accident.

I'm a paraplegic, I'm a full-time wheelchair user, and you can only imagine how complicated and how difficult and the number of obstacles it took for me to get back into the industry and really prove myself and show people that those with disabilities could work and bring value to the hospitality and wine industry. I had a mentor who's also a paraplegic. His name is George Gallego and we've done a lot of non-profit work together. We've done a lot of work for the community. He lives right down the block from Contento and he reached out to me. He knew that I really wanted to open a small wine bar restaurant and he said, Yannick, I think I have a spot for you that you might be interested in.

So, we looked at it and I said, oh my God, this is incredible. What was even more incredible was how inexpensive the rent was – very low. I said, let's do it, let's make this happen. The concept for it was that access was really important.

Firstly, we fitted it out and made sure that I could get there and roll in and roll out and serve the guests really comfortably and get behind the bar and make cocktails if I needed to. But secondly, to make sure that also the physical layout was comfortable for people with all types of disabilities. So obviously, people with wheelchairs, but also people that come in that might be part of the low vision and blind community and who have guide dogs and making sure that the guide dogs are also in a place where they're very comfortable, in a very safe place.

The third really important thing, and I say this all the time, you can create the most perfect, universal, barrier free, designed restaurant, but if you don't have that culture of empathy, if you don't have that culture of knowing how to deal with people, particularly people with disabilities, it means absolutely nothing.

People who have disabilities who come to us, it's unbelievable. I would say about 5 to 10% of the guests that come to our restaurant on a nightly basis have a disability, which is really incredible. If you build it, if you build that culture of welcoming, you're going to get people, they're going to come, and people with disabilities want to spend money. The reason why they don't go out to restaurants, or they don't support other businesses is because they don't feel welcome or the facilities haven't been built to make them feel welcome.

We're in no position, especially post pandemic globally - this is not just a New York thing or United States thing, but this is a global thing - I'm speaking to everybody - if you build that universal design, it's not going to cost you. It's not going to make you go broke. You will see a return on investment. Then, if you get some training, get people within the community, and teach your staff how to deal with people with disabilities, you're going to see a greater increase. What's better than to have diversity in your restaurant? That's what it's all about.

CC: What's the vision for the future now that we're hopefully heading out of the pandemic? Where do you want to go?

YB: The first thing I want to emphasize is that with Contento we certainly don't want to be known as the first restaurant who's putting a strong emphasis on making sure the restaurant is barrier free for all communities. I don't really care if we are the first or not, to be honest with you, because I don't want to be the last. I hope that other restaurants and other companies see this model and say, wow look at that, look at the work that they're doing and look how busy they are. Maybe they'll reach out to me and say, hey Yannick, do you mind helping us out with our concept because we want to improve our model?

We want to make sure that we're more inclusive. I think that's where the future is at. I hope that people will begin, and they already have to be honest with you, but especially when we go into the new year, to realize that, hey what they're doing at Contento, they're in this off the beaten path street, very quiet, there's lots of construction, but yet we get people from all over coming to us, from all backgrounds, so I hope that they reach out to us and say, hey, we would love to learn more about your model because we want to improve what we're currently doing at our restaurant. That's the greatest thing that can happen.

I want to just say one thing, too, one thing that really makes Contento so special, but it's not really mentioned. We have two investors that have a disability. They are our class B, whatever, behind the scenes, but they have a disability. Then you take myself, George Diego, and we have two other individuals that work at Contento who have a disability. We're a small restaurant and six people that are actually involved with the Contento project have a disability. That's really amazing. That says a lot.

CC: Your dedication to supporting people living with disabilities extends outside of your restaurant. Tell me a little bit about Wheeling Forward and Wine on Wheels.

YB: It's been incredibly challenging the last two years since we had the shutdown in March of 2020. It's amazing because it's going to be two years, and I can't believe the end of the year is right around the corner, but I'm excited about the first quarter of next year.

There's something that I'm developing, it's called the Solera Project, and with this project we're going to be hosting people with disabilities, and we're going to have them on the table, and we're going to be serving some food and serving some wine and there'll be a specific conversation, a theme. It could be wines of South America paired with food of South America.

Along with that conversation, we'll talk about current events that are happening in that specific region. One of the biggest issues that I see happening in our community of people with disabilities, is that they're not getting the kind of stimulation, they're not getting the kind of information that they need to be able to succeed in the workforce, so that's what we want to do. We want to be able to give people some information, conversational pieces, but again, feeling stimulated. Then the conversation will have people who come in who will lead maybe a class on resume writing, or how to save money.

What we really want is to create these individuals and build them up and hopefully other restaurants, other companies, maybe even wineries or wine companies will join us and take on some of these individuals that we're training as paid interns or even possibilities where they can work with them because people with disabilities really want to work, and they have so much to offer, they really do.

CC: Along with the outreach and building these programs, what's your actual role at Contento now? You are the beverage director, but what else are you doing

there that's making you excited to get up every morning?

YB: Well, listen, when you have a restaurant, especially when you have a small restaurant, and especially during this time of COVID, where it's really challenging to find people, the labor force, it's a challenging time for the hospitality industry, globally as well. I talk to people in England, in Italy, in France. Trying to get people to work full time and be dedicated at the restaurant is certainly a challenge.

CC: Sure. And people are frightened, too. There's a fear element. There's a lot to deal with mental health wise, as well as two years of having sat at home by now.

YB: Absolutely. Well said. I completely agree with you. And some people have what you call an invisible disability, a compromised immune system, so I completely understand that. But in my case, I'm what you would call the beverage director. But many nights I've had to take a station, work as a waiter. I've had to work as a host or maître d' to see people, which is what I do a lot of and then also getting out in the community and networking and keeping the restaurant relevant and being your own spokesperson and PR person for the restaurant itself.

You really have to be a Jack of all trades if you're going to own a restaurant. The idea that you'll just be one title and that's it, you're going to just set yourself up for failure, you have to have the ability to be able to do a lot.

I don't know what I am, but I love wines from all around the world. If it's good, it's good. The most important thing that I try to do with the wine list, there are some wines that are very geeky, but also making sure that there are wines that are recognizable for other people who might just like a good Malbec from Argentina or a nice Cabernet Sauvignon or Merlot from the West Coast of California, things of that nature.

There's a really incredible mix. We have wines from Lebanon, Morocco, Israel, Georgia, Armenia represented on the list. We have a strong representation of Italy and Spain. I love those wines, and, of course, France. If you look at the wine list, the one thing that I get complimented on is how incredibly eclectic it is. They like the titles. I have different titles for each section. It's not the traditional sense.

The first section of the wine list is called Wines of Impact. These are wines made by people from either marginalized communities or wine makers that are really conscious of the environment, that are really having either a social or an environmental impact. We have one winery on the list, I'll give you an example very quickly, it's called Keyshore Vineyards, and they're out in the Galilee, out in Northern Israel, and everybody that works on this winery, except for the wine maker, has an intellectual disability, so they employ people with intellectual disabilities, so they have a sense of purpose, a place to go to, and they're being productive.

That's just an example of taking an agricultural product, taking a product that we're also passionate about, that we love, but also it's having a positive impact on our society. With the non-profit work, it's been in hibernation for the last few months, but we're going to go back at it full blast. Coming January, we have a facility called the

Access Project, which is going to be a couple of blocks away from Contento restaurant. The facility is going to be a wellness and physical fitness center for people with disabilities. That's where we're going to be hosting a lot of the Solera Project classes.

I think we will bring people from all around the world, people here in New York, some chefs, it'll be sommeliers, people who work at wineries. It's going to be a mixed bag. It's not going to just be limited to just wine itself, but we'll have classes on beer, classes on sake, non-alcoholic drinks, the anthropology and social aspects of how food and wine and beer came about and how they impact society.

A lot of interesting conversations and guest lecturers from major universities that have financial backgrounds as well, along with people that are in law, things of that nature. It's going to be a mixed bag, but it's all about empowerment for a community that is often forgotten and doesn't have the resources given to them so they can succeed.

Luckily, I have a long list of potential students and partners from my years of being part of the non-profit of Wine on Wheels since 2012. Then I'm collaborating with my dear friend and partner at Contento, George Gallego. We have a very long list of names that we know of, people that are really interested and are flirting with the idea of perhaps being involved with the hospitality and wine industry, so we'll be reaching out to them, but it won't just be limited to people in New York. We're also going to have people who might live in California or any part of the world and have them zoomed in if they want to be part of it. It's not just a New York or an American thing. It's a global thing. We want people who have disabilities to succeed from all around the world, from Italy to France to India to Thailand to you name it. We want this to really be a barrier free organization. Finally, I just want to tell everybody to stay calm, breathe, push forward, because you're never too old to dream and believe in magic.

The takeaway

> **"Creating barrier free spaces is more than just a design issue, it must be accompanied by a culture of empathy. Entrepreneurs should be spokespeople for inclusion and education inside and outside their professional spaces."**

Conversation VII

EPISODE 891 – LAMAR COVERT

The audio

The issues

Including Lamar Covert's episode in the book was an easy choice. His drive to bring wine to people in his community in a fresh new way, in a space where they feel comfortable, and share his passion and experience is nothing short of inspirational.

The guest

Lamar Covert is from Philadelphia. He's the CEO at CYL Hospitality Group, handling many accounts, and catering and events management. He is a certified sommelier and a partner at BlacOak Wine Club, which opened new premises in Philadelphia in the autumn of 2021.

The conversation

CC: How did you get into wine? What was your road into the sector?

LC: How did I get into the wine industry? Working in the nightlife and the hospitality space, in my demographic, there was a lot of spirits, there was a lot of sweet liquors and things like that. As I got older, I began to dive into it, probably around early 20s, honestly, just curious about it. My life pretty much changed.

One night I was on a date, and there was an African American guy, he was well groomed, he was on a date as well, actually he was on a date with two women. So, in my early 20s, seeing that, I said, wow how can I do this one day, right? Aspirations. Right! So, the only wine at that time that I was drinking was a Sauvignon Blanc, a mass-produced Sauvignon Blanc, Cavit, Barefoot, Yellow Tail. He had a glass of red wine, and I asked the waiter what type of wine he was drinking, and he told me it was a glass of Merlot. So, I ordered that glass of Merlot, just trying to seem as if I knew what I was doing because I was on a date as well. I got that glass of Merlot and my life changed.

Throughout my early 20s, all the way up until now, mid 30s, I was drinking red wine for a long time, and I just went down a wormhole of research at that point. I would go to the local liquor shop and I would buy Merlot and one of the sales representatives one day said, listen if you like Merlot then you would like something like this. They suggested Cabernet Sauvignon and I began drinking Cabernet Sauvignon and I stopped drinking Merlot. I just went down a wormhole of drinking Cabernet Sauvignon at that point.

What really did it, I was in New York one time, at a small wine shop, and I was with a group of people, most of them were women at the time, so I was showing off a little bit, right? I asked the guy for a wine suggestion. He asked me on price and I said, well $50. I never spent $50 on a bottle of wine – ever! I was just showing off, making it seem like I knew what I was doing because I was so curious about wine at this point, I figured if I spent $50 I'd get a better bottle of wine. He asked me what I drink and I told him I drink big, full-bodied wines like Merlot and Cabernet. He said, listen try this, and he gave me a bottle of Bordeaux.

It blew my mind, right? It was a whole new world. It was a whole new world. It literally was like going to another country and never seeing any of the scenery. He gave me this bottle of Bordeaux. I think it was a Château Lafitte Haut-Brion. On the ride back home, I was literally glued to google about Bordeaux.

I went on a journey. I went on a trip. It was all I could think about at that point. So, yeah, this was probably around 2008, I want to say 2008/ 2009, probably. I just went down a wormhole to research every article I could find, every YouTube video, every book. I would just buy everything, and also the wine itself, and we know how expensive that can get. I just bought a lot and I would just sit in the house and read. I would sit in school and be at work just reading and Googling and tasting wine and trying to understand these tasting notes and aromas and things like that, which I didn't grasp until I went to school.

That time that I did that research on my own, it prepped me for when I went to school. I felt comfortable being in school at that time because I did five or six years of research before I even took a class. That led me to take online classes. I took some free online classes as well, just out of curiosity, and I've been on this journey ever since.

I went to the Wine School of Philadelphia. Instructor Keith Wallace is a renowned sommelier, a wine consultant and wine maker. He created the curriculum for the National Wine School, NWS, which is basically an accreditation agency just like CMS and WSET. He also started his own wine school in Philadelphia and through visiting wineries in Pennsylvania with my sister Ebonie, we had made a relationship with some winemakers and we would go so much and we would taste wine so much, I would have conversations with these winemakers.

One day he said, listen man, every time you come here we have these in-depth conversations. What do you do? Are you in the industry? And I'm like, no, I only do catering and events and things like that. I'm not actually in the wine business. He said, well how do you know so much about wine? I said, listen man, I'm just enthusiastic about this and I have a deep thirst for knowledge about wine. This was not something that I grew up with, and I'm just truly interested in it. He said, well listen, and he was very blunt and he's Caucasian, he said listen, for people to respect you in the industry you should go get your sommelier certification. He says, I'm going to be honest with you. It may be off putting to some people who do not look like you when you begin to talk about wine, he says, so I would never want anybody to belittle you or undermine what you're saying. You should go get the paperwork to back up what you're saying.

Because it was good advice, I didn't take it harshly. I didn't take it the wrong way because I had already developed a relationship with this guy. We were really cool at this point, so I took it positive. I took it as if he wanted me to prosper in the industry and he didn't want me to be taken advantage of or he didn't want people to view me a certain way because we know the wine industry, it can be very elitist at times.

So, I did it. I am certified sommelier. I'm in progress of becoming an advanced sommelier probably by the fall of 2022. I would be an advanced sommelier by then. So, yes, I'm still in school.

CC: Are you doing it with the Court of Master Sommelier in the States?

LC: I'm taking my advance with the same school right now. They have a master program, but their master program is more focused on business, if you want to start a wine business. I'm not sure if I'm going to go the Court of Master Sommelier (CMS) route. The level of knowledge that I have obtained from NWS and the Wine School of Philadelphia, I view it as being on par with other accreditation agencies.

I know a lot of people who are sat at CMS, and they also did WSET. We have these back and forth, these conversations, and it just reassures me that, okay you actually know what you're talking about. You actually got the proper knowledge on par with the other accreditation agencies. So, yeah, I don't know. I always thought about going faster, but it's just not in the cards for me right now.

Do I want to go to CMS? I'm not speaking down on CMS at all, but if I can sit down and I have this thirst for knowledge that I have, I just want to do this research on my own. Every book that has been recommended in the wine industry, I have that book in my house. So, if I want to just obtain this knowledge for myself and for me to be able to move forward and start a wine business in the future, I can do that on my own. I'm weighing my options at this point. Do I want to go that far? We'll see. But I'm going to finish up advanced first, and then we'll see what happens after that.

CC: Your new venture is BlacOak Wine Club. It started up over a year ago, offering classes online, industry updates and listing black owned wine brands, and you're hosting a podcast, the Wine and Cheese Girls Podcast. Your sister Ebonie S. Dukes said a really cool thing. Ebonie said, "the biggest thing for me is being able to educate people who look like me and make them feel comfortable walking into and being in rooms that may have been intimidating before." What are your goals for BlacOak?

LC: These wineries that we were visiting right when I met my friend Brian, who gave me this information, we were actually in the process of getting a wine produced by this winery. Throughout these conversations of getting this wine produced, Ebonie just called me one day and said, hey we're finding out about a lot of these black owned wine brands, and we are of the Support Black Movement, the Buy Black Movement. She said, listen we should start this wine club. Literally it was a five-minute call, she called me really fast.

Ebonie, she's a doer, she's a go-getter. I was probably in the midst of doing something else. She called me and I'm just like, yes, okay, all right, let's do it. Let's do it. Getting back to whatever I was doing and literally maybe 48 hours later there was an LLC, there was a website being produced. It just took me and my other partners by storm when this happened. The purpose of it is to expose black-owned wine brands, black-owned wine makers, black people in the industry, but then also educating our community about wine.

One thing that we began doing was in-home tastings and we were doing online tastings, especially because it started in the pandemic. We had to start whichever way we could at the time. One thing we realized is that a lot of people from our communities, and when I say that I'm talking about black people, we don't grow up with wine. A lot of us, we grew up with spirits in our households. Probably the thing that we had that was closest to wine was like Manischewitz.

We don't have a lot of wine knowledge. A lot of our families did not own land. They weren't vintners. Also in our communities, they don't market wine, they market spirits, they market sweet liqueurs. So wine was something that we weren't privy to. What I realized is that when they taste wine, they get turned off and they believe that that's what all wine tastes like. If you've been drinking cognac or whiskey or vodka, once you take a glass of wine, you're like, oh I don't like wine.

CC: You have to recalibrate your whole palate.

LC: Exactly. It's 1400 varietals in the world. Every wine doesn't taste the same. We felt like one of those barriers to entry was education, educating people about wine, how to taste it, how to smell it. What it looks like with the mouthfeel is, all of those things. Hopefully that will allow or encourage people to buy more wine, because if we're trying to get people to buy wine and especially with BlacOak, get them to buy black-owned wine, you have to be educated before you would even take that step to even search out a black-owned wine brand or search out wine itself.

Most people go to the local liquor store and they buy the thing that they always buy, what they're used to, what somebody else told them about. So, there's a lot of levels, a lot of walls to knock down when it comes to wine education in terms of the African American community.

CC: BlacOak is creating a community that strives to help the industry respect the buying power of black consumers and the expertise of black wine professionals. At the moment, only roughly one in every 1000 winemakers in the U.S. is black. And of the 11,000 wineries in the US, less than one percent of them are black-owned. The thing that's interesting for me is that the first recognized black winemaker was a man called John June Lewis in the 1940s in Virginia. What happened? Because clearly he was not leading the charge, or somebody made him stop. What happened? Why do we have so few black winemakers and black owned wineries?

LC: My knowledge, what I've researched, what I've talked about, there's a lot of discriminatory practices towards black farmers. When you think about the disadvantages of events like the Homestead Act of 1862, where there's no redistribution of land, nor were there any reparations after slavery, just various discriminatory accidents, black farmers and forms of federal policies, financial lending and just blatant, violent theft of their land. We were set back. We were set back. That plays a role when we start talking about land.

Even now with winemakers who own wineries, who may not own land, getting distribution for small wineries, that's very hard. Sales representatives, the loans that you may need to take out to even open a winery, let alone purchasing your grapes, getting your equipment, getting your workers, employees, a lot of it, I believe, stems back to being set back so long ago with the level of racism that black farmers have had to endure.

Land is one of the main sources of generational wealth within families. It's hard for these wine makers to get visibility outside of their local territories, like I said, with distribution. That's why we are now just getting to the point where you begin to see these black-owned wine brands. A lot of the black-owned wine brands don't own the land, they're just wine makers.

It's going to take a while, but I feel like we're getting there. We're on track, especially now within this last year, of course, unfortunately, with George Floyd, which pretty much sparked the Buy Black Movement. A lot of the black winemakers now have gained national distribution because of that, because everybody is speaking about them on social media. Some of these black-owned winemakers, they're getting national press.

Last year made it evident that black people have a power. There's a power in our voices, and that power and our voices has pushed these black-owned brands to the forefront. Hopefully it's not just a trend. Hopefully people stick by it and continue to support it. Certain wines, certain black-owned winemakers, they can't make certain wines because of where they're at or the access to certain grapes, but as time goes on, I'm sure they'll figure it out. We'll figure it out as time goes on. I just hope it's not a trend, I hope people just inform you.

CC: Aside from BlacOak, what is CYL Hospitality Group doing? Are you partnering with black-owned wineries for your events, for your catering things? Because you're wearing two hats, you've got BlacOak and you've got CYL. What are you doing with them?

LC: Yes, CYL has always been my baby. I've always wanted to be in the hospitality industry. I've always had goals of opening a restaurant, and I have a lofty goal of operating a hotel at some point. So that has always been a goal of mine. That one thing that you have always thought about in life. That always was in the back of your mind. That was it. Hospitality was it. I love hospitality. I love to accommodate people and make people feel good, which is probably why I was in the nightlife industry at that time, being able to provide people an experience, provide them a good time. So right now, with CYL we pretty much took the approach of catering to just begin to put ourselves out there and allow people to experience what we do. We're going to launch this summer some wine pairing dinners and I will be reaching out to some black online brands. But again, just having wine, period, I think is great with these pairings because people begin to see different types of wine. There's no black-owned wine brand that makes a Chassagne Montrachet. So, I still want people to be able to be educated on Italian wines and French wines and other wines. But that's definitely a part of the program that we will be putting together. Hopefully one day we'll be having another conversation, and I'll have a hotel that I can invite you to.

The takeaway

> **Recognize the barriers created by racism and elitism and encourage and support removing those barriers through education, innovation and opportunity.**

Wine, Food & Travel

MARC MILLON

Introduction

Wine can be elite, exclusive, expensive, or else it can be "of the people, by the people, for the people". The latter is what interests me most, exploring and discovering the democracy of wine in Italy in all its varied and many aspects. Since time immemorial, wine here has been the beverage of the people. Yes, kings and queens, emperors, popes, grand dukes, counts, *marchesi* and *marchese* have all enjoyed - and in some cases continue to enjoy - the fruits of the vine. Yet even so, throughout history and even pre-history, wine has always been the everyday beverage of ordinary folk too, the traders and merchants, farmers, peasants, *mezzadri*, servants and serfs, and, in ancient Rome, even slaves. I don't deny that there is undoubtedly an aristocracy of Italian wine, and quite rightly so, those superstar wine producers who deserve - and sometimes demand - to be treated like nothing short of royalty. And why not? They are the ones who have toiled over the past decades to help create and build the reputation for Italian quality wines, not only within Italy itself, but internationally and around the world. Interestingly, in some cases (though by no means all), a number of these same producers do indeed come from Italy's noble classes: princes, dukes, *marchesi*, counts and the like.

This should come as no surprise since, for centuries and millennia, wealth and prestige has always come from the land, from those expanses of fertile and productive agricultural countryside worked on behalf of noble and wealthy landowners by armies of nameless laborers.

Equally, however, and never more so than at the present moment, Italy's reputation as one of the greatest wine producing countries in the world has been created by families from humbler origins. Former *mezzadri* - sharecroppers just a generation or two ago - now rightly own and work their lands in their own names, producing scores of fabulous wines. In other cases, small growers have banded together to work collaboratively in cooperative wineries that are producing amazing award-winning wines. Social projects, too, serve to safeguard disappearing ways of life and communities, as well as to defend biodiversity and centuries old vines and vineyards.

Historically, wine has long been the preserve of men. Italian men were the winemakers, and they travelled the world bringing their wares to new markets and appreciative wine lovers. Today however, women have now taken their rightful place in the world of Italian wine, as wine producers, business owners, enologists, marketeers, communicators and sommeliers, their talents recognized, applauded and appreciated, their stories finally told, or just waiting to be told.

It is always interesting to delve into the past, and the story of wine in Italy is one that dates back centuries.

Following the fall of the Roman empire and the subsequent spread of Christianity, viticulture and winemaking continued through the Dark Ages, in no small part through the diligence of hardworking monks, a legacy that continues in historic wineries today. Elsewhere, on the shifting mudflats of the Venetian lagoon, island communities reclaimed the land and established themselves as farmers and fishermen, where the cultivation of the vine was as important as it always was on *terra firma.* These and so many other stories are fascinating chapters in the never ending and compelling story of Italian wine. In Italy's wine democracy there are literally thousands of winegrowers, and hundreds if not thousands of wine producers, each with their own unique story to tell. "Wine, food and travel with Marc Millon" gives me an opportunity to meet these mainly small growers, discover their origins, and to uncover where they have come from and where they are going.

Wine quite simply lubricates daily life in Italy, the natural accompaniment to meals for people across all social classes. It is the drink of celebration in good times, and it consoles in moments of sadness, too. By meeting and speaking to producers about their wines, the foods that go best with them, as well as the places where they live and work, we gain a precious insight that goes far beyond the wineglass, a window into their personal lives, their culture and history, their way of living, indeed their very identity. Through the simple act of sharing a glass of wine, a plate of food, we celebrate the universal, communal and democratic bond that unites us all as human beings. This is my vision of wine democracy.

Conversation VIII

EPISODE 763 - MATTEO BISOL

The audio

The issues

The archipelago of shifting mudflats in the Venetian lagoon was originally settled by people escaping from the danger of marauding invaders from the north, the Germanic tribes that descended into Italy following the fall of the Roman empire. Little by little, lands were reclaimed from the sea, the islands and islets shaped and settled by farmers who cultivated the mineral rich soil, and fisherman who took bounty from the waters of the lagoon.

Eventually, the Maritime Republic of Venice grew into an empire of merchants and seafaring traders who came to control the entire Eastern Mediterranean. Yet farming and viticulture remained an everyday activity of the Venetians with vineyards cultivated even on the main island of Venice itself in the various *campi* or squares throughout the watery city. Meaningful viticulture on the lagoon, however, virtually ceased after the great flood of 1966, which destroyed the vineyards along with much else. At that time, it made little sense to replant vineyards, as plentiful wine was so easily and readily available on the nearby mainland. And yet, and yet, it seemed that something of the soul of the islands was lost when viticulture ceased.

Thankfully, a visionary winemaker, Gianluca Bisol, of Prosecco Bisol in nearby Valdobiaddene, dreamed of restoring viticulture and wine production to the lagoon. Through his faith and considerable efforts this has now been achieved with the Tenuta Venissa project.

Bisol and his team were able to rediscover an ancient and historic grape variety, Dorona, that not only has unique flavors, but which is able even to survive *aqua'alta*, the regular flooding of the fields with the brackish, saline waters of the lagoon. On the island of Mazzorbo, a vineyard has been planted and in the surrounding buildings, once part of a monastic complex, a luxury hotel has been created with a Michelin-star restaurant that specializes in a simple and pure island cuisine utilizing almost entirely the products of the Venetian lagoon. It might seem strange that the wine that has resulted from this project, Venissa, bottled in a beautiful hand-etched 50cl bottle with hammered gold leaf label that has been fired in the furnaces of Murano, produced in limited quantity only and subsequently very expensive, is an example suitable to represent what "wine democracy" means to me. But it is wholly fitting, for Venissa represents something of the true soul of Venice, a celebration both of Venetian artisan craftsmanship, and also a celebration of the simple people of the lagoon, those farmers and fishermen who first settled here and went on to create one of the most magical and evocative places on earth - Venice. Matteo Bisol shares the fascinating story of the Venissa project.

The guest

The 22nd generation of a family of wine growers and producers, 34-year-old Matteo Bisol became general manager of Venissa in 2013. The company includes a vineyard of the native grape variety Dorona, a Michelin-Starred Restaurant, an osteria and a wine resort. With a background in business studies and a deep passion and knowledge of the wine world, Matteo brings his clear vision and values to the project, putting purposeful tourism and sustainable viticulture and gastronomy at the core of his efforts. Matteo's proactive work in promoting the integrity and authenticity of his native Venice goes hand in hand with his role as custodian of the natural and cultural heritage of the northern lagoon.

The conversation

MB: So, the Venetian lagoon is quite a big lagoon. It's composed mostly, obviously, of water and there are hundreds of little islands. Mazzorbo is in the northern part of the lagoon, close to the island of Burano, which is famous for its colorful houses. There's a bridge connecting Burano and Mazzorbo, and it's also close to Torcello, which is the island where Venice was actually founded 1500 years ago.

MM: So Mazzorbo itself has a long history, although it's not an island most people have heard of. It too was important at the beginning of Venetian civilization in the lagoon, wasn't it?

MB: Yes, it was. There used to be around 20 churches in Mazzorbo, just to understand how big the island is. Actually, the name itself perhaps derives from *maior urbs* (biggest city), as there were actually thousands of people living in that area. It was the place where Venice started. Then around the year 1000 people moved from that part of the lagoon to Venice, which is actually about 30 minutes away by water taxi, but at that time, it took a little bit longer because there was no engine in the boat. It was quite a journey to reach Venice from Mazzorbo.

MM: Sure. And it's still an adventure. I know it's a very special place to come to. I've come by the vaporetto, the slow boat, but the nicest way is to come on one of those sleek and beautiful and very fast Venetian taxis.

MB: Yeah. It's quite convenient to reach Mazzorbo from Venice and it's a very beautiful journey to be on a boat on the lagoon. That's definitely an experience that I recommend to anybody that travels to Venice.

MM: Definitely. Now, what's interesting, you've mentioned all of these islands, these small islands, large islands around the Venetian lagoon. When we tend to think of Venice, we think of the main island of Venice. But these islands once had agricultural products growing on them and still do. Viticulture used to be prevalent. Perhaps there were vineyards even in Venice itself, but viticulture died out. What happened?

MB: The history of viticulture in the Venetian lagoon goes back 2500 years. Even before Venice was founded, the Romans used to have vines in the lagoon. So that's a very long history.

We really need to understand that the islands of the lagoon have a completely different history compared to Venice itself. Venice is a city which is really based on trade and merchants, everything is based around that.

The lagoon has a completely different culture. It's a culture based on nature. People always lived alongside nature, thanks to nature. Obviously, water was very important. The fishing village of Burano, which is near Mazzarbo, also the land and the soil was very important because Mazzorbo and Torcello, and then also Sant'Erasmo, Le Vignole, other islands in the same area, people always lived with nature, because they used to be poor people.

First of all, they were growing their gardens, they were cultivating the land that was available. If we look also at the names of the island of Venice, there's an island in the area which is called Le Vignole, which means vineyard in Italian. Actually, there's an island which is now called San Francesco del Deserto, because San Francesco came there, but before it used to be called the island of the two vineyards, Isola delle Due Vigne. There are other names that remind us of this history of agriculture and especially viticulture in the lagoon.

We really need to understand that making wine in Venice, agriculture in Venice, is not something strange, but is actually part of the tradition of the city. It's very important to preserve this tradition, because viticulture and making wine in Venice is completely different to making it in any other place in the world. The systems that have been invented by the Venetians to raise the vine in such an environment where you have high tide and all these challenges only exist in Venice. This is really part of the history and the patrimony of the city. It's very important to maintain this history alive.

MM: Well, that is really fascinating to put it in that

historical context and to think of what the challenges are making wine from grapes, from vineyards that, as you say, have to be able to survive *aqua alta*, the flooding. Normally a saline brackish water flooding onto a vineyard would cause great damage. How come that doesn't happen with your vineyard on Mazzorbo, because I know it can flood at times, can't it?

MB: Yes, the vineyard was flooded in the big 2019 *acqua alta*, and we were very worried about the consequences of this because we know that it's a very dangerous phenomena. The *acqua alta* was in November and until April we didn't know if the vineyard had survived or not because it was winter, and the vines were sleeping. In Venice a grape variety exists, called Dorona di Venezia, which is a local grape variety. This local grape variety adapts itself to survive in this environment.

You know, the vine is an amazing plant, in Italy we have more than 1000 different grape varieties. The reason is that each grape variety adapts itself to a special environment, to special conditions of the soil, of the weather, of everything that found a place where it's living.

Dorona di Venezia adapted itself to survive in the lagoon. It's a grape variety that was almost extinct because when we started in 2002, we only found 80 Dorona di Venezia vines in the lagoon because there was a very big flood in 1966 that damaged Dorona. But losing most of the vines, created a lot of opportunities for tourism, in Murano, glass factories.

Being a farmer in Venice was very difficult. It was also expensive to grow things in Venice and with the motorboats, it was easier to transport things from out of

Venice than in. In that time, during 1960s, 70s and 80s we lost the tradition of viticulture and agriculture in the island of Venice. We were lucky enough to find some of the last farmers of Venice, especially Gastone Vio, who was still growing some vines of Dorona.

Then actually, we were finding vines of Dorona almost everywhere. Maybe one vine in the center of Burano island, a few vines in Torcello in front of the basilica, some vines in Le Vignole, even in the places where we're growing actually today in Mazzorbo, and our neighbors also has Dorona. So, we collected 80 vines and we reproduced it by *selezione massale* method, and we were able to replant to the vineyard in Mazzarbo.

MM: Wow. That is a fascinating story of how this particular grape, unique to the lagoon was preserved. It would have been lost if the Venissa project hadn't found a way to keep it alive. The extraordinary thing from what I've tasted is that it's a grape that's not only able survive, but that produces an extraordinary wine. That's a fascinating part of it. Tell us a little bit about the wine itself, because it's unusual.

MB: Yes, it's a white wine. It's a white grape variety. Somehow in each vineyard this grape variety is related to other grape varieties. If we need to place Dorona in that scene, we would place it in the families of Trebbiano - Garganega. These are quite neutral grape varieties that reflect very well the terroir. Our vines are varieties that can produce wines that are completely not interesting in terms of quality, but can also produce some of the greatest white wines in Italy. It really depends on where the vine is planted and how the vine is grown.

We will have incredibly different results if we think about the Trebbiano di Valentini or some of the Soave. These, I think, are really some of the best Italian wines. But Trebbiano grape varieties are also used for mass production wines. It's very important that Dorono di Venezia is in its own environment, the Lagoon of Venice, because I always believe that it's not a matter of having a special grape variety. It's not that Pinot Noir makes great wine everywhere in the world. Pinot Noir makes a great wine for sure in Burgundy, Riesling found itself perfectly in Wachau and in Mosel, and Nebbiolo grows perfectly in Piedmont. But we don't have examples of great Nebbiolo somewhere else in the world. So, it's not only a matter of the grape variety, but it's always about how the grape variety found the perfect symbiosis with the terroir, and Dorona di Venezia found a perfect symbiosis with the lagoon of Venice. That's very important because it's allowed us to produce a very balanced wine, a very elegant wine, a wine with obviously a great personality, because the terroir is quite unique. The grape variety is different. We're talking about a white wine which is produced with a maceration on the skin. There's also a historical motivation behind that. The reason is quite simple: in Venice, there was no possibility to build an underground cellar. With the risk of the high tide, if you build the underground cellar, this would be flooded. Underground cellars were very important in the past to produce a quality wine because it allowed to keep the temperature low during the summer. So, the Venetian had to go around this problem and to find a solution. Venetian people are incredible.

They found a solution to many problems to build a city in the middle of a lagoon. It's the same thing with the history of this wine.

They found an incredible system to grow a vineyard, and they found systems, obviously, also to make the wine.

Maceration was the solution, because with maceration you were able to extract the tannins and the antioxidants that are in the skin. This allows the wine to survive and last longer, even if it's not in a perfect condition during the summer, even if the cellar gets a little bit warmer than a normal cellar. Maceration was really the tradition of making wine in Venice, and we kept this tradition, obviously, also for our wines.

We make a maceration that lasts around 30 days, one month for the Venissa and around one week for the Venusa, which is the second wine of Venissa. We keep the wine in concrete tanks for a few years and we release the wine only around four to five years after the harvest, because these wines really need the time to express themselves, these are wines that can age really well. If we have to drink the best Venissa wines today, we would need to drink 2010 or 2011 vintages.

MM: It's a wonderful wine and I had the opportunity to taste it at Venissa, so I can really understand what you're saying. It's a white wine made almost like a red wine in that sense, with this long maceration. It's become, in a sense, a symbol of the Venetian lagoon and of the heritage of the lagoon, reflected in the beautiful bottle and unique label. Tell us a little about this and why you decided to present the wine in this way.

MB: The reason that brought us to produce a wine like

Venissa was not just to produce a wine, but to restart and keep alive the tradition of the lagoon. As well as the tradition in the lagoon of Venice of producing wine, there are other amazing tradition of handcrafts. Some of them are related to glass. We all know that the island of Murano is very famous for glass. We felt that in this project there needed to be a place for the hand crafters of Murano. We don't produce the glass in Murano because that's artistic glass and otherwise the cost and the price of the bottle would be amazing only for the reason of the glass, but we wanted somehow to have it on board. Dorona means the golden grape, this is the translation of the name. In Venice there is a family that is called the Batiloro, the goldbeaters, representing the last family of a tradition that is almost extinct. They make the gold leaf with a hammer, and they have this amazing tradition that goes back to centuries. They are now the last families doing that. And we are the last producer of the gold grape. We wanted to somehow try to keep both the traditions alive and to help this tradition to become more well known. On the island of Murano, the gold leaf is baked into the glass. There's a family that is specialized in applying the gold leaf to the bottle, to the glass. They actually cook the gold leaf inside the bottle. They etch "Venissa" and the bottle number on the glass.

The takeaway

> **Support policies and encourage businesses who are engaged in the conservation and preservation of vulnerable ecosystems and historic viticultural practices.**

Conversation IX

EPISODE 917 - LUIGI GAGLIARDINI

The audio

The issue

After the Kingdom of Italy became a unified state in 1861, parts of the country experienced significant changes in the system of land tenure. In some places, feudal rights were abolished, large rural estates were broken up, and significant tracts of land owned by the Church were sold off at state auction. As a result, a new class of small landowners emerged together with tenant farmers who now had the right to profit from the toil of their own endeavor. It was mainly to them that a new form of cooperative venture was most appealing. The cooperative movement grew out of the need and the desire to find a way to help these small farmers to grow, transform and market their produce. The basic idea behind the early cooperatives was to find a way to create businesses or organizations that were owned and run jointly by their members for their mutual benefit rather than for the profit of landowners or shareholders. Today, no less than 60% of Italian wine is made in cooperative wineries, much of it of very high quality. Indeed, at the 5-Star Wines and Wine Without Walls Awards that took place at Vinitaly in 2022 wines produced in cooperative wineries gained some of the highest accolades. Terre Cortese Moncaro, a cooperative in Le Marche, for example gained Winery of the Year and Best White Wine awards. Luigi Gagliardini, himself a wine-growing *socio* of the cooperative, tells the story.

The guest

Luigi Gagliardini is the director of sales and marketing at the Terre Cortesi Moncaro winery in Le Marche, which won winery of the year and best white wine at 5-Star Wines and Wine Without Walls Awards 2022

The conversation

LG: Putting into words, the beauty of the landscape and of the nature and the philosophy of the wine is the job of the poet and I'm not a poet obviously, but I'll try my best. I'd like to introduce Moncaro first of all because it's important to note that we are a co-op, not a privately owned company. We are an ensemble of farmers who come from the area and which was founded in 1964 here in Montecarotto. Montecarotto is one of the castles around the city of Jesi that gives the name to the famous appellation, the Verdicchio di Castelli di Jesi DOC. Castelli di Jesi in English means castles of Jesi, so all the castles around the main city of Jesi. Montecarotto, where Moncaro is located, is one of those castles. It's a little town on the top of a hill, which was once an old medieval castle, which became a small town. There are two thousand people living there and there are 20-25 of these little towns around the area. It's a hilly area with vineyards all around, as well as other kinds of cultivation. It's a beautiful landscape which goes from the sea towards the mountains, the Apennines, so it's very gentle, coming from the sea towards the mountains, and we are in the middle on the hillside.

MM: That's a really good vivid image, these beautiful rolling hills topped by the Castelli di Jesi and then the proximity of the Adriatic Sea and the high mountains of the Apennines. An important thing you mentioned Luigi, it's not intensive monoculture in Le Marche, is it? You have this beautiful patchwork of vines, fields of wheat, sunflowers. Just a beautiful mix of countryside.

LG: Actually, I can't say exactly the historical origins, but this was a Vatican state back in the day, with lots of different cultivations and deep agricultural roots. Very different compared, for example, to Tuscany where you have much less cultivation, more forest and more villas. You know, basically the rich people who were doing trade in Tuscany probably were taking the foods from here, where we were all farmers making food for them in simple words.

MM: Yes, that's really interesting. I guess you're talking about the time when the *mezzadria* was still in force and people cultivated a bit of everything because they had their own self-sufficient small holdings.

LG: Exactly. That was until very recently. That's one of the reasons why there are so many co-ops in Italy. In our case, the emancipation of the farmers from the *mezzadria* law led to the birth of the co-op movement as farmers sought emancipation from the *mezzadria* law where you had to basically give away half of the cultivation to the landowner. More often it was much more than the half of it. To be more self-sufficient, people started to gather together, get together and decided to create their own company for selling their own products, being more self-sufficient and living a better life basically. The government and the region helped the farmers in achieving such a great objective for their life and the co-op has been a very important part of this. Since the very beginning, the main objective of the co-op has been sustainability. Everybody is now using the term sustainability, but sustainability, in terms of economics, social, and life in general, has been the main objective of the co-op since its foundation. Giving a better life to the farmers until today where we are a competitive company in the global markets, but still the main foundation is the sustainability of the life of the people.

MM: Okay. So, the small farmers who wouldn't have otherwise been able to produce wines on the scale that we're talking about, the quality as well, the co-op, the idea of banding together to produce something collectively, is very, very important. Italy is actually a very cooperative nation as a whole with this philosophy.

How many *soci* do you have? How many cooperative members who are growing grapes?

LG: Almost 60% of the total wine in Italy is made by co-ops. In our case, we have about 800 members and a total of 1,200 hectares in three main areas, because we have three different wine cellars where we produce the wine. One is here in Montecarotto, which is the headquarters and the main cellar. As well as another one in Camerano, which is by sea, at the bottom of the Conero mountain, which is a nice-looking promontory which goes to the Adriatic Sea. The third winery is in Acquaviva Picena near Ascoli Piceno. Those 1,200 hectares are in those three main areas and allow us to produce all the appellations from the region. Let me also tell if I may that I am so proud to be a member of the co-op myself with a small vineyard which is here in Montecarotto. Working for a co-op you must have a little bit more motivation, which goes beyond the economic recognition of your work. It's a little bit more of being, it might sound a little bit rhetorical to say, but part of a big family and you're doing the good of the farmer, so that's the main objective of the co-op.

MM: Through these cooperative values and through the work of the farmers you've been able to achieve this winery of the year award, but also white wine of the year for the Verdicchio dei Castelli di Jesi "Fondiglie". Tell us about this wine, this award-winning wine, this expression of Verdicchio, which I think is one of Italy and the world's great white grape varieties and yet it's only found in Le Marche.

LG: Exactly. It is. They tried to cultivate it in other areas in other regions, but with very poor success. It's a grape that is rooted here for many, many centuries. It's fair to say that it's the most flexible kind of grape in Italy, because you can do all kinds of wines very successfully with this grape, from very fresh aromatic wines to more mature, to sparkling wines. There's a very strong tradition of sparkling wine making here, and also sweet wines. You know, we made a wine which was chosen a few years back to be drank at the Nobel prize dinner in Stockholm. You know, they have this gathering of 4,500 VIPs and they had to choose sweet wine from all the wines proposed from all over the globe and they chose our Verdicchio.

MM: Wow, that's incredible.

LG: Yes, you can do all kind of wines with Verdicchio. It's a very well-structured grape, with big shoulders and it can do pretty much anything. It also has great aromas if you treat it in a certain way. Getting back to Fondiglie, the wine which got this very nice award, Fondiglie is the name of an area here. It's a *cru* basically, and it's an area in the town of Rosora, which is one of the castles of Jesi, and it's pretty high. It's about 350 meters above sea level. That allows grape to get lots of acidity and lots of structure yet with the great primary aromas of the Verdicchio. In this wine we were able to make a product which is, on one hand, very structured, very persistent, and, on the other, very aromatic. So, a wine which could sustain any kind of pairing, which you could drink without eating anything, by the swimming pool. Eclectic and very elegant and persistent and mature from this small area which we have been cultivating since forever.

On the label we have the design of a bee on a flower because on the vineyard there was an old farmer's house and the old farmer had written on the wall a poem on the wall of the house. It is an old poem about the bee, which goes flower by flower. The poem goes something like this: "happiness is a small thing like the bee, it just picks the flower and goes".

The takeaway

> **"Recognize the value of co-operatives for maintaining the economic, social and environmental viability of rural communities."**

Conversation X

EPISODE 695 - EMANUELA FLORE

The audio

The issue

Italy's timeless patrimony of old vines is something that needs to be preserved for it represents not only the toil and efforts of several generations past, it also embodies disappearing ways of life. Furthermore, old vines, in some cases ungrafted and more than a hundred years old, are capable of producing fabulous wines that have flavor and texture not found in younger plants, albeit produced in extremely low quantities.

The guest

The Bentu Luna project in the heart of Sardinia serves to safeguard and preserve such old vines by empowering families of small winegrowers as stakeholders, a way not just to create great wines from vineyards that would otherwise be abandoned but also as a means of preserving and maintaining traditional culture and a way of life and living that otherwise might also be lost. Winemaker Emanuela Flore is from one such family and she tells her story with CEO Gian Matteo Baldi.

The conversation

MM: Gian Matteo, can you tell me a little bit about the project, how the project began and what is the ethos, the reason behind doing what you were doing?

GMB: Well, the project began a long time ago and it took a long time to be digested. The idea is Sardinia is in the middle of the Mediterranean and is one of the places where viticulture in the Mediterranean started. So, we're talking about a culture which probably has more than 3000 years. Right in the middle of Sardinia, you can find the same kind of vines that they had 3000 years ago.

There is a long-lasting culture and I think it's a patrimony for everybody. Unfortunately, in the past, of course, old vines which belong to this kind of culture, produce less and therefore revenue for the people who were cultivating these vines was getting smaller and smaller. Since the vines are passed from generation to generation, the first generation left to find some other job to sustain the agriculture. We are now in a situation where the grandfather can't pass it on to their grandson because there wasn't enough revenue.

The risk was that this huge patrimony, we're talking about more than 1200 hectares of old vines, would slowly disappear. So, the idea was, first of all, that it would be a pity to lose that kind of patrimony, then there is a big social damage and, last but not least, you

can make amazing quality wines from these grapes. So, from there we started to develop this project.
EF: This project puts them, the men and women, at the center of the project. In their day-to-day life, they participate in the project, they grow and they make something which probably they have underestimated because it was something taken for granted. Through the project they have a different perspective and a different opportunity for the future.
Basically, this kind of cultivation has been there for 3000 years and, as long as our civilization doesn't change, the commerce and globalization, because most of this production was made for the family. The family would produce their own wine or olive oil, the cattle and everything. Now everything is different. For them this was something which they had in their culture but maybe they forgot the powerful sense of having been years in their family. So, through this project they are more self-conscious and through the daily work they do, they're getting closer and closer to something which has been passed on down the generations, even if they hadn't realized what it meant.
MM: I tasted the wines today and I was so impressed with them. They had such concentration and richness of flavor in such a pure, clean form - ***Complimenti*****! Tell me a little bit about the old vines themselves.**
EF: What we're living with now with these old vines is the result of choices that were made in the past. On the one hand, we know that the people that came before us, our ancestors, they had such a strong wisdom about the quality of the soil, the microclimate and everything,

they'd been experimenting for so many years. So, they really knew the value …

MM: This knowledge was passed down generation to generation.

EF (in Italian): On the other hand, there is the reality of Sardinia, which is an island in the middle of the Mediterranean. Many people came to the island, and they brought new ways of doing things, new cultures…

MM: Even new grape varieties.

EF: The result is this, a blend of culture and knowledge. What we have now is the blend of this culture and this wisdom and this knowledge. So, the story we are telling now, the wine we are making now, is the real story, our story. It's the story of the island. The taste represents our history and who we are.

MM: A taste and flavor that could come from nowhere else on earth.

GMB: I think so.

MM: Let's talk about these native grape varieties that are most important for you. I know you're growing only grape varieties that have been on Sardinia for a very long time.

EF: The three basic ones are Cannonau, which is Grenache, Monica and Bovale, which are the main red varieties in the island. Together with those, there are many other varieties which are blended with the other three to represent the territory. Each of these small plots of vineyards, they were family vineyards. Each family had his own recipe, and each family had its own creativity. Maybe the grandfather brought back from some variety and the other decided that he didn't like that one. Also, they used to like to compete on the quality of the wine. Each one of these family vineyards had a particular recipe with a small addition of one variety or another. That's why you can find up to 17 up to 18 different varieties in a single vineyard.

MM: I want to clarify how you work with these families, because this is a very interesting part of the project. How many families are you working with now?

GMB: We started with eight and now there are more than 25.

MM: More than 25. And these are small holdings that have been traditionally in families for generations.

GMB: Yes.

MM: The grandparents would have worked the land, but the next generation couldn't make a living from it, so now you're working with the grandchildren. So that's a beautiful continuation of a way of life as much as a continuation of a particular wine.

GMB: We didn't want to buy the vineyards, we rent the vineyards so they can stay in the family. That gives them revenue and a reason not to abandon the vineyards and not to decide to dismiss them. In general, the father lost the opportunity. They went away. They looked for a job, many of them decided to do other things. But the grandchildren, I think, if they didn't have this chance, most probably they would lose the possibility to continue the tradition, the knowledge, the vine training and the vine cultivating. This kind of culture has a huge effect on the old vines because, apart from the fact that they're less productive, you need to have a very good viticulture to allow a vine to survive 120 years. You really need to understand the plant, the way you prune it, because otherwise the vineyard would die much earlier. That's what happens in a normal vineyard, usually after a few years they tend to get too old. So that kind of culture is very important to continue.

We have at least twelve young people, the oldest is 35, 36, and they work in the vineyards and they're learning. Through the project, their understanding, knowledge passed on by words, now they also have a scientific reason to what they were doing, so they have a better understanding of what they're doing.

MM: Emanuela, to make wine from your ancient vineyards with the knowledge that has been in your family for generations, but now with your scientific training as a winemaker: was it your dream to make wine in this way?

EF: This project gave me the chance to fulfil a dream I always had, to create a new perspective for these vines and to make a wine with a new taste, which could represent Sardinia all over the world.

MM: It's linking an old tradition with a modern mentality.

GMB: There are some very innovative aspects to this project, something which could be replicated elsewhere. For example, now most of the wine producers are very involved with the concept of storytelling. I want to sell the wine, I need to have a story to tell. We do not have a story to tell, in a sense that going so deep in details, inside the project, is the story. We don't need to invent a story to tell, we are the story. That really simplifies it for us. Telling this story to a customer or a client and having these people taste the wine is a perfect cycle. It really works.

MM: Tell us a little bit about this Vermentino wine, which is fermented in terracotta amphora.

EF: The idea was exactly as you said, having spontaneous fermentation, having an even stronger element to represent the territory where the wine comes from, even with the yeast. I believe that my role as a winemaker is to find a way to transform the grapes into a taste which is the most authentic interpretation of the soil and the region.

MM: Can you talk to us about some of the red wines that you produce from these great varieties? Cannonau, which is more well known, particularly when we know it as Grenache, but also the Bovale and the Monica?

GMB: Yes. We actually make four different wines. Two are basically the expression of two different crus. One is Mandrolisai, which is a DOC of the area, a plateau between 500 and 700 meters high. The other one is Neoneli, which is a small area just next to it, but it's different. They are the blend of up to 12 to 15 different vineyards, but they are made in exactly the same way. When you taste them, you really taste the difference of the soil and the terroir. The other two wines are two single vineyards. The reason we decided to bottle them by themselves is, firstly, because it's made only with Cannonau, or Grenache, because that family decided that was the best grape to use for their wine. So, we kept it separate.

MM: So, it's a single vineyard from a single family.

GMB: It's a single vineyard from a single family. We

found no reason to blend it with the rest. And the other one is another single vineyard. We decided to keep it on his own because it's so distinctive, because it's a vineyard which was planted in 1905. After phylloxera it was grafted, probably one of the very first grafted, before the nursery system came along, there is a huge biodiversity and the same Cannonau / Grenache inside the vineyards, you might find four or five different biotypes, the Monica and the Bovale, and grapes that we don't know even the name. It's like tasting something which is coming from another time. That wine is called Be Luna, which means moon wind or wind of the moon.

The takeaway

"Ancient cultures, like ancient vines, need to be carefully nurtured to prepare them for the future, blending tradition with innovation and technology."

Conversation XI

EPISODE 1014 - ERIKA MARCHESINI

The audio

The issue

The *mezzadria* was a system of sharecropping prevalent particularly across central and northern Italy whereby a peasant farmer - a *mezzadro* - and his family were supplied with a small house - a *casa colonica* - and a patch of land, on the condition that half of what was grown and produced would be shared with the landowner. The *mezzadria* not only came to define social relationships between worker and landowner for some 800 years, it also shaped and defined the very countryside itself. As each *podere* had to be self-sufficient in order to support the *mezzadro* and his ever-growing family, a system of mixed farming known as *coltura promiscua* - promiscuous cultivation – was favored.

Each plot of land was divided up into sections, perhaps a few rows of olive trees, a patch of grain, a vegetable garden, three or four rows of vines, an area to keep the chickens or the pigs, and so on, depending on whatever they were cultivating. Vines were sometimes trained onto trees or other living supports to free the land below for other crops, a method that had been used since Roman times.

This medieval form of agricultural was so successful (admittedly most successful for the landowner) that it was only phased out as recently as the 1970s. Thus, today many of Italy's most successful and interesting small wine estates are run by the children and grandchildren of former *mezzadri*, sharecroppers who just a few generations ago had been working for someone else but had somehow managed to find a way to acquire land in their own name for the first time. Here Erika Marchesini shares the story of her family wine estate in the Bardolino wine hills above Lake Garda.

The guest

Erika Marchesini is the voice of the Marchesini Family winery. Along with her sister Giorgia, she has been running the family winery near Lake Garda since 2014. Erika is the public face of the company, responsible for managing client relationships in Italy and around the world. She also organizes on-site wine tasting experiences with a personal touch.

The conversation

MM: Tell us a little bit about where you are, about the Bardolino area. Describe it because our listeners would like to have a picture of this beautiful landscape with the beautiful Lake Garda on your doorstep.

EM: I'd love to. I hope to be able to take you here on hills of Lake Garda. Here we have a particular climate. A Mediterranean climate. So, it's a perfect place to grow vines and, of course, live. You said a little bit about the pergola Veronese, which is our main training system.

We love the pergola, of course, because it has a special climate. The bunches on the pergola Veronese hang on the plant. So they are protected by the leafs. Of course, the breeze of the lake helps us to keep the vineyard air conditioned because it keeps the bunches fresh and dry. This is the most important thing, especially during the summertime, because we know that the dryer and fresher the bunches are, the healthier they are.

MM: That's very interesting because in the past decade some producers were deciding to not use the pergola Veronese because it's very labor intensive, isn't it? It's hard work, reaching up to harvest those bunches.

EM: The problem, it's not a problem exactly for us, but the pergola Veronese is expensive. It takes a lot of investment in terms of effort, time and, of course anytime you work on the vineyard, it's time, and of course money. But at the same time, if we keep the pergola, if we grow the grapes in the right way, if we make the selection of the grapes, if we keep the vineyard in good condition, we from the pergola we can obtain very high-quality grapes. Of course, at this moment the branches are protected by the leaves, but when later in August, normally in mid to late-August when the days start to became a little bit less hot and nights start to became a little bit fresher, we can start leafing so the bunches will receive a little bit more sun.

MM: Now, Erika could you tell us a little bit about the history and tradition of the Marchesini Family winery? How long has your family been involved in winemaking?

EM: The business started with my grandfather Plinio

in 1970. My grandfather was a poor farmer. He was a sharecropper for the Count Cavazzocca. He worked as a sharecropper for many years and in the 1950s he was able to buy the Santi vineyard, where he had worked as sharecropper, which he was really proud of. Ten years later, in the 1960s, he bought the vineyard here at Valesana where today we have the cellar. Close to the vineyard is our house which had a small underground cellar. From that moment, he decided to transform his passion for wine making into a business. The 1970s and 1980s were a very good time for Bardolino wine. It was an important Italian table wine. He started the business at the right moment. He was good at wine making, for sure. He started selling this wine, selling the Bardolino all over the north of Italy. He delivered the wine door-to-door with his truck. Ten years later, in the 1980s, my father, who had been working in other local wineries decided to join my grandfather. They worked together for almost 30 years, because fortunately my grandfather worked until the last hours of his life. Today my sister Georgia is working alongside my father as the wine-maker. She worked in other local wineries, and then decided to start to work here with my father. Today, she is leading the vinification in the vineyard. I'm more front office, because I'm leading the relationships with our importers, with our customers, the wine tastings of course, and all the office jobs. All the family is working here, including my mother. We all help with everything.

MM: That's a really beautiful and important story, Erika, to hear how from the 1970s this is the *mezzadria* you're talking about. The family had been sharecrop-

pers, as you said, perhaps cultivating a little bit of everything because you were a self-contained little farm then. Then your grandfather was able to purchase land and become a producer in his own right. That's an important chapter in the story of Italian wine as well, because it was such a social change when the *mezzadria* was stopped, and it's not that long ago, we're talking about just a couple of generations. Then the winery was built up by your father and now the next generation is there, so it's a really important story for that continuity and for the wines. Let's talk about the wines, the grapes you grow then, and the wines that you make.

EM: We are based in the Bardolino wine region, in Lazise, in the Bardolino Classico wine region. Our main grapes are four autochthonous grapes: the Corvina, Corvinone, Rondinella and Molinara. The Corvina and Corvinone are the queen grapes of Verona, they are our favorite grapes to give spice and red fruit notes to the wine, but at the same time we all love a lot the Rondinella and the Molinara, which are mineral grapes. We use them both for Bardolino and Chiaretto. These two wines that are brother wines, because they are obtained from the same grapes, are fresh and fruity wines. They are mineral wines because the minerality that comes from our soil, from the particular soil we have here on the lake.

MM: We're talking about a similar *uvaggio* or blend of grapes as in Valpolicella, but it's that *terroir*, that soil, the rock below the soil that makes a different style of wine, a lighter red, would you say? Bardolino I think of as a fresh and delightful red, mainly to drink young.

EM: Yes, sure. The terroir makes a real difference between the Valpolicella and the Bardolino, of course. Bardolino is a light ruby wine. When you put the glass of wine against a white paper, you can see through this wine because it's transparent. I love to say that it's like a person who has an open heart, an open mind, because it is really easy and elegant, but it's really a wine that is like a friend because it's honest and it's really a unique wine. It has certain characteristics. It's easy to drink. You can enjoy a glass of Bardolino, a bit fresh in the summertime, especially during these hot days. Of course it is a wine to enjoy, not only very, very young, because it has a four, five years of potential aging, for sure. But we love to enjoy it within a couple of years from the harvest. The Bardolino has a brother, the Chiaretto, containing the same grapes with the rosé vinification. The Chiaretto is the young and fresh brother of the Bardolino.

MM: Okay, so the Chiaretto is a rosato, but quite a full colored rosato, is that right? Is that how you make.

EM: The rosato is lighter paler than rosé. It has some pink and pale shades, but it's not dark. It's a very rosé, very rosa color. It has a color that's really lovely. We decided to offer this wine with a twist cap to keep this color as long as we can, because the rosé wines are very delicate. They can change color very quickly. This is why we need a hermetic closure. The twist cap is to keep the color as long as we can.

The takeaway

“Respect the contribution of previous generations and the social and political context in which they built the foundations of today’s viticulture. New generations can build on those foundations to create a more sustainable future for viticulture.”

Conversation XII

EPISODE 806 - ROBERTO STUCCHI PRINETTI

The audio

The issue

History and wine are always intimately linked in Italy. Following the fall of the Roman Empire and the subsequent rise of Christianity, the Catholic Church became an important landowner in its own right, as wealthy families, eager to secure the best place in *Paradiso*, donated tracts of land to the Church. Through the Dark Ages, viticulture was furthered and enhanced in monasteries across the country that produced wines not only for use in the daily sacrament of the Eucharist but also as an everyday beverage for the monks themselves, as well as for the lay community and for travelers and pilgrims who passed their way. If the former Vallombrosan abbey of Badia a Coltibuono, in the hands of the Stucchi Prinetti family since 1846, is no longer an ecclesiastical institution, you can, nonetheless, still gain an insight into how a self-sufficient monastic smallholding supported not only its own religious community, but also gave hospitality to passing guests and pilgrims. The fine abbey still stands at the heart of the property, now transformed into an elegant family villa with cloister, corridors, frescoed rooms, as well as accommodation for guests in restored apartments and individual bedrooms transformed from the former cells of the monks.

The Restaurant, located in the former stables, is highly regarded for its traditional Tuscan *cucina*. The wines of the estate, certified and cultivated organically, are simply outstanding, brilliant expressions of Chianti Classico at its finest. Roberto Stucchi Prinetti, winemaker on his family estate, relates the story of a fascinating and historic place.

The guest

Roberto Stucchi Prinetti is the General Manager and Winemaker of Badia a Coltibuono, an organic wine, olive and forestry estate in Tuscany. Starting in 1985 he directed the organic conversion of the estate. In 2016 he was a co-founder of the Biodistretto del Chianti. As president of the "Biodistretto del Chianti" he works with the local administrations to expand organic practices to all of Chianti.

The conversation

MM: I have very fond memories of visiting the Badia a Coltibuono. Can you please describe for our listeners your wonderful property and the surrounding countryside so that they can gain a visual impression, an image of where your state is located?

RSP: Yes, Marc, as you said, we are a very historical winery property. We are on the southeastern hills of Monte del Chianti, in the forest close to the summit, overlooking the Arno Valley at about 630 meters of altitude. We look north into the Arno Valley, the valley of the river that goes to Florence, facing the Apennines. We're in the higher part of Chianti, but the estate is divided in two parts. Our vineyards are actually a little bit further away, also in Gaiole but at lower altitude in the zone of Monti at the southern edge of Gaiole. The estate is really two different parts. Where the monastery is, what was the monastery, we have the agriturismo, the aging cellar, the restaurant, and it's at high altitude. Then we have the winery and vineyards in Monti at the opposite edge of Gaiole. Two very different parts of Chianti, which is very diverse, so we embrace two sides of it.

MM: The Badia has a long and illustrious history going back many centuries. Can you tell us something of the history of your estate?

RSP: Yes, it's an amazing place. This was a monastery

founded by San Giovanni Gualberto, protector of the foresters, in 1051. He founded a monastery on the Apennines called Vallombrosia, which gives the name to the Vallombrosian order, who were a spinoff of the Benedictine order. They were looking for a more pure monastic expression. They were very involved in agriculture and forestry, which is why the founder, San Giovanni Gualberto, is the protector of foresters. They had a very important role in the evolution of medieval agricultural which, I always like to remember, for the first time in this part of the world, not only the monks, but a coherent system of what we would call sustainable agriculture was developed. They started terracing, they started using cover crop, rotation of cultures. They created what defined the Tuscan landscape for centuries, until very recently. The monks were there until 1810. That's when Tuscany (of course Italy wasn't unified yet) was annexed by Napoleon and the monastery was secularized. From that point on, it was a private estate, it had different owners, and our family acquired it in 1846. This is our Giuntini ancestors, and it's been in the family with lots of ups and downs ever since, for seven generations now. It's a large estate. The monastery was converted first to a villa and then to an agriturismo for farm holidays. We have restaurants and rooms and cooking courses. We also try to maintain and preserve this beautiful place, the building, but also the forest around it, the vineyards, olive groves and everything else.

MM: It's very interesting what you're saying about sustainable agriculture, really dating back to the origins of the monastery. I guess that would have been the

mixed promiscuous culture as opposed to monoculture that we find today, under the m*ezzadria*. Is that what you're talking about? When Tuscany, the landscape itself, was very different from what we see today.

RSP: Right, exactly. The m*ezzadria* was also a kind of social revolution, because the farm workers were basically serfs, slaves before that and the monks by the system where the family who farmed the land had control of half of the crops, so half the crop went to the owners of the land and half to the people that worked there. This was a very socially advanced system for the time and a big evolution. That, paired with better techniques of farming, which the monks introduced because they had access to the Roman manuscripts. They reconnected with classic culture and built on that. So yes, the *podere* was the farm unit with all the parcels of forest, farm forest and was used to raise the animals part of the year, but also mixed crop. Very similar to what, interestingly, what I would call postmodern agriculture, like permaculture, it looks very similar to what a *promiscuo toscano* was and has been for centuries. Three crops alternated with ground crops, integrated with animals that would graze and keep the land clean and fertilized. It was a very productive system. The land produced a lot. Interestingly we think of modern industrial agriculture as high yielding, but if you look at how much food was produced in a small parcel of land with that system, it has something to say. Obviously, a system that didn't survive modernity, but now some parts of it are being rediscovered.

MM: In fact, the productivity goes to the actual name of

the estate, the Abbey of the Good Harvest - Coltibuono. So, it's been a productive farm for all of these centuries?
RSP: Yes, absolutely. At the peak it had about 40 *poderi*, 40 farm units within the property. We still own a good part of the land, but most of the farmhouses were sold in the early twentieth century or mid-twentieth century when times were very difficult. Some of them are now independent estates nearby like Capannelle. They of course have their own brand name, but yes, a lot of land. Chianti had a much higher population than it has now. In the 1950s and 1960s a lot of people left, but these farm units hosted very abundant families, large families. We had about twice as much population in Chianti before the Second World War than we have now, even after 30 years when there's been people moving back in the area. At the lowest point, we were down to one quarter of the population of the 1970s, so big changes in Chianti.
MM: That's really interesting to hear how social changes happened as that ancient agricultural system was phased out. Badia a Coltibuono also has this long history of hospitality. The monks used to offer hospitality to travelers, to pilgrims. Are you actually located on the Francigena, the important medieval pilgrim's route that went from northern Europe to Rome?
RSP: No, we're not. The Francigena is more west of us in the lower area, closer to Siena. The Monte del Chianti was actually a secondary route. It was quite important. It's named Cammino Micaelico, after Michael the archangel. That's why there were a series of monasteries on this path. Basically, the road from Florence goes

south, it's actually a beautiful walking path. If you have good stamina in seven or eight hours you can walk to Coltibuono from Florence, all on the top of the Monte del Chianti. Along you'll pass near Badia a Passignano, which is still a monastery, Valle Ambrosia, and then the remnants of Montescalari and then Badiaccia a Montemuro. So, there is a string of monasteries. I've heard, and I haven't found a very strong historical evidence, apparently this was a route that was used quite a bit in the summer. In the winter there was too much snow and the Francigena was more viable. But in the summer it was actually healthier up on the hills because some of the lower areas had swamps and malaria. so sometimes this was popular during the summer months.

MM: Returning to the sustainability of this ancient system, but also of the farm today, you were one of the pioneers in the Chianti Classico in conversion to organic viticulture. Can you tell us a little bit about this and what challenges it posed you and, indeed, the state of organic viticulture in the Chianti Classico today?

RSP: Yes, you could say that we were early adopters of organic practices. I grew up in Milan, studied agriculture. While I was studying agriculture, this was the late 1970s, I did a course in biodynamic agriculture. I had no idea what I was getting into, but the oldest biodynamic farm is near Milan in Italy. I never really embraced the whole spiritual side of biodynamics, but it taught me a lot about complexity and how to learn about the health of a farming system which starts, of course, with the soil, biodiversity and everything. I studied in California for a few years in the 1980s and I learned a lot from local farmers who were beginning to embrace organic. Not so much wine makers, wine joined organic movement a lot later. When I started at Badia in 1985, I immediately went in that direction. The big challenge back then was little information, little support from academia or science. The agricultural science was still very much inorganic. There was no attention on microorganisms in the soil or biodiversity, so it was treated more like an industrial system, where you put inputs in and you get things out. Now, of course, it has evolved and the situation has changed a lot. There are now a lot of people that are doing organic. Chianti Classico today is over 50% certified organic with a lot of biodynamic and other advanced forms of organics, permaculture and whatnot. It's developing really fast, which is nice. Now there's a community. I'm also President of Biodistretto del Chianti, which is a specific association of organic producers. It's nice to be working together on this and it's much less lonely and, of course, you can do a lot more when you can work on it together, that's the recent development.

MM: That's very encouraging to hear, and an extraordinary high proportion - 50% - I'm surprised to hear that. Is Chianti Classico an area that lends itself to organic in terms of not having the risk of some of the maladies that would happen in moister or more varied climatic areas?

RSP: Well, up to a point, yes. Organic works better either way, even when you have difficult conditions. If you're trying to grow grapes in an area that's really not well suited, it's always going to be up hill, whether you use organic or conventional techniques, you will still have a hard time. One of the concepts behind agroecology, which is the basis of organic and biodynamic and everything else, is also to grow things where it makes sense to grow them, so in that sense, yes, Chianti is very well suited for vines. But, I would argue that even if you are growing a crop where it's not well suited, you're still better off using organic practices, because healthy soil means the plants are healthier and easier to protect.

MM: Are there younger people now returning to the land?

RSP: Yes. At least trying. It's not easy. We have an issue, for example, with too many wild boar and deer. That's a real problem these days and hard to manage, but yes, there is certainly a lot of people coming back. For decades, Chianti focused pretty much on wine and that was good because it brought it back from a very difficult period. Now more and more other food crops are being grown again for local consumption. That's really nice. It's very important for the future and for the health of agriculture. There's a lot of space to do that if you can manage somehow the wild animals, that's a real difficult part.

The takeaway

"The future can sometimes be found in the past, as experience and farming methods based on respect for the land and the soil are rediscovered, offering sustainable solutions and attracting younger people back to rural communities."

Conversation XIII

EPISODE 736 - TERESA SEVERINI

The audio

The issue

Women's rights, stifled under fascism, came relatively late in Italy. Full suffrage was only granted after the Second World War, prior to 1970 there was no provision for divorce in Italian law, and abortion was not made legal until 1978. Wine is part and parcel of Italian society and indeed a reflection of society. Only a few decades ago, the wine sector was an activity, a profession, a métier reserved almost exclusively to men. But the world and Italian society has changed and today women now take their place amongst the most talented winemakers in the country.

Indeed, women are more closely involved in all aspects of wine than ever before - not only as winemakers but also as marketeers, administrators, communicators, journalists, expert tasters, sommeliers. This is reflected in the organization *Le Donne del Vino*, which brings together women in the world of wine in all its varied aspects. Its various concerns and activities include campaigning to improve working conditions and rights for

women in the wine workplace.
One of the pioneering women in wine in Italy is Teresa Severini Lungarotti, who was in fact Italy's first qualified female winemaker. Here she shares her story and the story of the iconic Lungarotti family wine estate in Umbria.

The guest

Teresa Severini was Italy's first fully qualified female enologist. Now Director of Marketing and Communications at the Cantine Giorgio Lungarotti Winery, she is active in the work of the Lungarotti Foundation, and a founding member of "Le Donne del Vino", an association that promotes the work of women across the wine sector.

The conversation

MM: First of all, I'd like our listeners to get a real idea of where you are in Umbria because it's a very special place.
TS: Umbria is a region right in the center of Italy. There is no coast, it's inland. Torgiano is close to Perugia and Asissi, just to let you know a little bit about the famous places. Torgiano is a small medieval village. Easy to reach? Not so much, but difficult to leave because when you come you live so well it's a pleasure to stay.
MM: The entire wine zone of Torgiano didn't exist until your stepfather, Dr. Giorgio Lungarotti, came to the area to establish a new wine with a new mentality. He was really one of the pioneers of the modern renaissance of Italian wine. Can you tell us a little bit about this family story and how the region has developed?

TS: Yes, he was really a pioneer. He was a visionary and decided to give a new life because he understood very well, he graduated in viticulture, so he understood that the place had great potential. He had to change things from the tradition. The wines were already known for being nice wines, but he wanted to create great wines. So, he started to work the land, changing a little bit the way to cultivate the vineyard. When I say a little bit, I mean a lot, because there were a lot of revolutions in the wine field, in the vineyard, in the winery. He changed a lot, but he was humble. He wanted to travel before creating all these changes. He travelled a lot, to France, Germany, other countries, to see what was creating a difference from the tradition here. He started a new age. He was the first in Umbria. As a matter of fact, we received the first DOC in 1968, the fifth DOC in Italy and later one of the very first DOCG. That's the proof that what he thought to do was right. It's so easy to think of changing the styles and so on, but go back to the 1960s, the late 1950s, early 1960s. It was really like a revolution. People would say, this man is mad, but he was right. Together with my mother, who formed a great couple, they started to talk about wine and about culture, and this made a massive difference. They also paid great attention to specialized tourism of wine, today we call it *enoturismo*, but at that time it was attracting people based on wine to a territory which is so beautiful and so dedicated to wine production.

MM: It was visionary in so many respects. We have to remember that, in the 1960s, the countryside itself was completely different. This was the time of the

mezzadria, **of mixed cultivations, there wasn't a specialized viticulture.**

TS: Yes. Giorgio was one of the first to close the *mezzadria* contract, and he re-employed all the people, the *mezzadri*, as employees. He formed an *equipe*, very close to him, with us too, because we have the children of them working for us again, the continuation of dynasties, shall I say?

MM: You were the first female oenologist when you qualified in 1978?

TS: Early 1979. I worked for three years on a technical basis on the ageing of red wine, that's why I graduated in 1979 instead of 1978. This was really something shocking because it was not a female field. For many years I've been the winemaker here, but I also took care of the promotion abroad. Then more and more I moved to the marketing and communication sector. Now I'm increasingly involved in the Lungarotti Foundation because I'm so fond of the fact that culture and wine have to go together.

MM: We'll talk a little bit about the foundation and activities in a moment. I'd just like to draw attention to some of your flagship wines, wines that I've been very fond of over the years, in particular, the cru wines, the Torre di Giano Vigna il Pino and the Rubesco Vigna Monticchio. Can you tell us about these? The Rubesco certainly is what people think of first when they hear the Lungarotti name. These are wonderful wines that are amongst the great wines of Italy.

TS: Yes, I agree. This year we won the first place, together with a Sassicaia, for the best red wines in Italy with the Rubesco Reserva 2016. This was a source of great pride for all of us. For my sister, for me, for Chiara. Remembering the passion that Giorgio put into this wine and also the passion of all the young people working here, because this is another point that I have to emphasize, this is a young winery, and that's very important, a lot of enthusiasm and a lot of work went into this. So, the placement for the Rubesco Reserva was fabulous. But you're right, Torre di Giano Vigna il Pino, which is the white counterpart of Rubesco Reserva, is a great wine. I remember Edmund Penning-Rowsell writing about this in 1980. He was drinking a 1970 of this wine. He wrote an article on this saying, "I was astonished to see how an Italian white wine can not only last for ten years, but even grow in these years". That's the real thing. It was before the fashion of white wine in wood. It's partially in wood, but at the same time, it keeps flavor, elegance and body. The wood is not overpowering, not at all. This was going back many years. Today it's still the same wine, fantastic for wine lovers, it's a couple - Rubesco Reserva and Torre di Giano Vigna il Pino. On the label you have a particular detail of the Fontana Maggiore in Perugia, which I love. It's the most beautiful fountain of the square from the thirteenth century. Again, it's a link between art, culture and wine that goes back many years with this label.

MM: These are two wines that are flagships of Lungarotti, and they also celebrate the traditional grape varieties, the Sangiovese, Trebbiano, Grechetto.

TS: Absolutely. We have experimented with clones and so on for many years. We think that, of course, the quality is already settled in the vineyard. So, you have to find the right place for the variety and then obtain more and more and more. That's what Giorgio gave us as a statement and a legacy, and that's what we do. For many years we have been very close to Denis Dubourdieu [French winemaker and professor of oenology at the University of Bordeaux]. Unfortunately, he's no longer with us, he died a few years ago. He's a man that I respect with all my soul. When I studied in Bordeaux for my specialization, I met him, his wife, the family. I found a great personality in wine, also a great friend. After Giorgio died, Denis started to be our consultant. He started to give us a new idea to continue the revolution and I thank him for having a lot of suggestions. So, we still have the Italian style, but with a deep attention to the soil, to the vineyard.

MM: Really expressing the terroir of Torgiano.

TS: Now we have another winery in Montefalco. There it's different because Sagrantino is a special grape, so different to Sangiovese. The land is also different. Thanks to our experience in the vineyard, on the soil, we kept the right way to grow Sagrantino, which is not too aggressive but very pleasant and round. That's what we like on the wine. To be pleasant, to be drunk and not only a glass, but an entire bottle.

We have many different kinds of wine. Wine is something that you have to match with your food, with your occasion. It's not only one kind of wine, but many. We also have San Giorgio, for example, which is a combination of Sangiovese and Cabernet Sauvignon. We have Aurente, which is a great Chardonnay. We have many-

MM: Yes. You have a wonderful range of wines, an

extensive range. What I've liked following the Lungarotti story is this blend of tradition and creating new traditions, new wines.

TS: I like this! Yes, I agree. We created new traditions.

MM: Now let's turn to the culture of wine and wine hospitality, because again you were pioneers here at a time when I remember when we were researching our Wine Roads of Italy book, which was in the late 1980s and came out in the early 1990s, you already had in place a really important complex of hospitality and culture through the Museum of Wine, which is one of the great wine museums in the world, extensive and important in not just showing how wine was made, but in placing wine in the context of culture and art. It's a beautiful project!

TS: It's something that everybody must know. First of all, it's not the museum of Lungarotti wine. The foundation has the mission to expand the culture of wine. The two museums, because it's a wine museum and an olive oil museum, are two art museums: creative art and the history of man. Talking about the wine museum, my mother always says the name "wine museum" is not sufficient to explain what it is, because really it is, of course, the history, the tools, etc., this is the part which you cannot avoid. You can find museums inside the museum. Let's say, for example, the ceramics. We have the most important collection of ceramics on one theme in existence, going from the Middle Ages to the Renaissance to the modern times. Then a collection of ancient printing, ancient because we go from Mantag-

na, for example, to arrive at Picasso. So, it's a long time period that is observed through more than 600 drawings or prints. Or we have the archeological findings going back to the third millennium BC, so 5000 years of history of the civilization of wine. We like to create a dialogue with modern exhibitions of art, contemporary art. For example, in this moment we have Andrea Tana, who is an American growing up in England and then in Paris and now in Umbria. It's so beautiful to see this dialogue because the concept is of a museum which is dynamic and talking different languages.
Of course, the wine museum is more important, but the Lungarotti Foundation is very active also in the education of drinking, the respect for wine and the sensibility of this. My mother has written different books, me too, in this field because the young have to be educated about moderate drinking. The second museum is the olive oil museum. It came very late because the wine museum was established in 1974 and then, of course, continuously updated. The olive oil museum was created after Giorgio's death, because it was a legacy from him to have another museum about this beautiful product of our land, extra virgin olive oil. My mother, a historian of art, she created the two museums by herself. She created the olive oil museum. As you said, the wine museum is considered the most important in the world, not only in Italy, because of the collection inside.
MM: Olive oil and wine have been there since the Etruscan times.
TS: Absolutely, yes. When you visit the wine museum and the olive oil museum, you can follow this long history of the civilization of this land. An experience is the

visit to the winery, of course, the tasting, but also visiting the wine museum and tasting the food all together. That's our feeling from the beginning.

The takeaway

> **“Focus on the power and creativity of women to do great things, and their ability to connect history, culture, art and wine.”**

Uncorked

POLLY HAMMOND

Introduction

Many perspectives, many voices

With so many walks of life represented amongst our podcast team, it's only natural that we would each define Wine Democracy in the context of our own personal values and professional interests. As a marketer, expat and parent, I look toward democracy as a system that (done right!) allows for representation, relevance, and resilience; that ensures that we become neither entrenched nor complacent; that gives hope.

Is it too ambitious to ask Wine Democracy to do the same – to help us evolve, open new doors, forge better connections? I think not. But the time to do so is now upon us.

From shifting consumer demands and saturated markets, to digital overwhelm and near-constant climate crises, wine is at an inflection point. Now more than ever, we need business, marketing and communication practices that move us beyond the status quo and give us confidence to take risks. This is my goal for Uncorked.

With this series, I encourage you to question wine norms created by class and privilege, as demonstrated by the success of Diva Giles, the GenZ owner of

an award-winning wine bar. I share inspiration from non-traditional business stories, such as that of Bordeaux-Nigerian wine mentor Chinedu Rosa.
I challenge notions of visibility and power, and who better to bring that message than the inimitable Cindy Gallop.
Featuring guests from within and beyond the wine world, Uncorked is there for anyone who seeks a resilient, adaptable, hopeful future for our industry. Let's get into it!

Conversation XIV

EPISODE 786 - DIVA GILES

The audio

The issues

This conversation focuses on how hospitality providers can appeal to a wider audience of wine consumers by offering an authentic and empathetic service.

The guest

Diva Giles is the co-owner of Beau Wine Bar, known in Auckland for its robust wine list and more-ish food, but most importantly, for being a hub for wine lovers from 18 to 80. With an approach that breaks the common rules of wine, she and her business partner Logan Birch have definite thoughts on how the wine world markets to and communicates with a younger audience. And if their success is any indicator, they're doing something we all could learn from.

The conversation

PH: Wine language can be very intimidating. How do your staff speak about wine with a younger audience? Do you find them wanting to use any of the tasting note style language all over the wine industry?

DG: We honestly ban it for our team. I've never understood it. Now I've got more experience and tasting wines constantly I get it a bit more, but we really reduce and talk about what the flavors are and how it makes you feel rather than the tick boxes of what's on the back of the label. It just confuses people and makes them feel like they don't know what they're talking about.

PH: We've talked a lot about what you're serving and what you offer. One of the things that I find interesting is that your business practices are very different from other local competitors, competing wine bars. You have opted not to use a lot of social media channels. You've got a pretty minimalist website. How have you grown the business?

DG: Well through people like you. It's really just word of mouth, you know.

PH: A lot of referrals.

DG: We didn't really have a budget for marketing. We spent all of our money on refitting the space and lockdown, so marketing wasn't really a thing. It was just about "we want to be local," we didn't want to be a destination restaurant. Our intention isn't to be on all the lists for the "best of" or even to win any awards. We're not looking to be the best, we just want to be your favorite. And I think the way to do that is, you know, create a sense of community and community grows when you add to it. So, it's people.

PH: I deal with a lot of businesses but, to be honest, most of them are owned by much older people than you, right? And the way that they communicate is often quite staid. I've noticed with you and your team that you are very open when things go wrong.

You're very values-driven and you communicate a lot of that on your social media channels, particularly on Instagram, where you will shut the doors because there's been a crisis. You will take time out for your team. You support your staff members if something goes wrong in the space. Do you feel like you're doing something different or innovative in how you're driving that business?

DG: I don't, or I didn't, until getting feedback from our community. What you're referring to was, we had one of our team members pass away last year. It was a shock and a surprise, and we closed down immediately, as soon as we found out, and then we stayed closed for a few days and that's us. We're a team of 17 people, of course, we were going to close. How couldn't we? I couldn't have worked, how could I have expected any of our staff to work? But I'll just say that it's really natural. Of course we're going to care about these people, of course we're going to try and provide balance for them, of course we're going to support someone when her father's passing away. Of course, we're going to be open with our customers about what's happening for us, because you want to be authentic and that's the only way to really operate, but for us it just felt natural, but the feedback that we've gotten in the last couple of years, I recognize that maybe it's not as normal. Younger generations, you know, now owning businesses are choosing to run and operate these spaces with empathy and kindness. And I think selfishly from a business perspective, that's how you then create a sense of community and how you also retain people and how you grow and create longevity and sustainability to people's careers within hospitality. So, there are two sides. Just do it because you're a fucking good person and you care and then do it because that actually makes sense for you long term. But maybe it's not going to work. I definitely have those days where I'm like, my god, maybe this isn't actually going to work long term, but I don't want to run a business if it's not going to be how we get to do it. Then I don't want to do it.

PH: You're a 26-year-old woman running a wine bar. Does that ever present problems when you're dealing with the wine trade?

DG: All the time, yes, particularly when we first opened. Often what happens - and this is across the board, and I imagine it's an experience you have all the time - is people just talk to Logan, my business partner. They'll just ask him questions and, you know, let him know things. That was really tough. Boys coming in and being like, "Where's the owner?" My team love it, the front of house women love it. They'll just be like, "This is the owner, this young woman." That's gotten better in the last years but that's just because we are working with the same people. Logan's really on board with that. As soon as someone comes in, it's really obvious that they don't want to talk to me or that they don't think I know what I'm doing and we just go, "Cool, thanks, bye." I mean you can have the best fucking Chablis in the world but if you're going to treat me like shit, then I don't want to do it.

PH: Last question. What if you had to pick one thing that everyone listening could do to actually just be better to our younger markets? What would it be?

DG: So, if I could pick one thing...

PH: No, actually, tell me as many things as you want.

DG: Stop talking down. You know, often people talk down because someone knows less than you and that's the quickest way to turn me away from a conversation. This person is just talking at me. They're not actually listening or learning or wanting to engage about what I'm looking for or what I know or what my life experience has been with wine. So, I don't know. Listening and actually just engaging. But I think it's even in hospo, just giving a shit about the person that you're talking to is the most important thing. In my opinion, that's the only way to be a waiter, to be a host, to run a business. The only way to sell wine is to give a shit about the person that you're talking to and actually engage with them. And talk to the humans, not the industry, and the concept and the wine. Empathy, the most important part of life.

The takeaway

“Offer a service that is authentic and empathetic.”

Conversation XV

EPISODE 840 - CINDY GALLOP

The audio

The issues

The voices of older women have often been marginalized from the wine industry. This conversation explores how that situation is now changing.

The guest

Cindy Gallop is a graduate of Somerville College, Oxford, whose background is over 30 years in brand-building, marketing and advertising. She launched the U.S. office of ad agency Bartle Bogle Hegarty in New York in 1998 and in 2003 was named Advertising Woman of the Year. She is the founder and CEO of IfWeRanTheWorld, co-action software launched in beta at TED 2010 and subsequently written up and taught as a Harvard Business School case study, which enables brands to implement the business model of the future — Shared Values + Shared Action = Shared Profit (financial and social). She is also the founder of MakeLoveNotPorn, a social sextech platform designed to promote good sexual behavior and good sexual values.

The conversation

PH: I'd love for us to dive into is the communication to grown women around alcohol, which also happens at a time when those same grown women are finding, because of menopause or pre-menopause, that they cannot drink the same amount that they used to.

How does an industry reconcile that we need to speak to these audiences, but then we also have the World Health Organization coming out and saying that any woman of reproductive years has no business drinking. We've got lesser alcohol consumption standards for women, as in literally the quantities that are safe drinking for women are far less than they are for men. So, it seems like just from sheer biology, we have a challenge talking to women, and we have a bigger challenge talking to grown women who have the money and the know-how to be good consumers.

CG: So again, I go back to my principle of communication through demonstration. You solve that very simply, and you kill two birds with one stone. You solve that simply by having a campaign that is a range of women who are menopausal, older women like me, as I said, talking about their individual approach to managing their alcohol intake. And then not only do you present women with a whole range of different approaches, and again I stress the campaign, the vignette, because I think the range is really important. A range is respectful. It says you can make your individual choice, but also you will break down the prejudice against talking about menopause by actively welcoming into this campaign menopausal women.

And I have to tell you, that would be enormously powerful because, for the benefit, again, of our listeners, first of all, you know, as Polly knows, I have been combating ageism for decades. I'm very vocal about, all manner of aspects which I live my life because I consider myself a proudly visible member of the most invisible segment of our society, which is older women. I want to help change through the way I live my life - again, communication through demonstration - what society thinks an old woman should talk like, work like, be like, and quite frankly, date like.

So, a couple months back I was asked to participate in a wonderful interview series on YouTube, Instagram, et al, run by a brand called Style Like You. Style Like You is run by mother-daughter team, Alicia and Lily, who have an interview series called What's Underneath.

In this interview series, they ask individuals and couples to basically sit on a stool and answer questions Alicia and Lily ask them and ask each person answers each question. They take an item of clothing because the whole idea is that both literally and metaphorically stripped down to what's underneath. So, they ask me to participate in a segment of the series that was called Defying Ageism.

So, at the age of 62, I took all my clothes off down to my underwear while asked a number of questions about my approach to life, love, relationships, etc. And I have to tell you that I was completely blown away by the extraordinary response to my interview. First of all, I went viral on TikTok, and I by the way I'm not on TikTok, but the clip of me on Tik Tok the last time I looked has 4.4 million views on TikTok and a whole host of Gen-Zs and millennials basically took my clip and created their own versions. There are 900 versions of my interview on Tik Tok, which shows you, by the way, how much an old woman can role model for young people. And the comments on YouTube all kicked off on Instagram are extraordinary.

There are so many young women, especially, saying Oh my God, I am desperate for older female role models, strong, confident women expressing surprising, unheard views. In fact, that there was one comment on Instagram and it's one of the videos I found very moving. The woman said, "Imagine if we had all grown up seeing and hearing women talk and live like this. Think how very different our lives will be now." That's the answer. Communications through demonstration.

PH: We see that all the time with brands. We're working with a big American brand right now on some communication where it is very much directed to younger women. One of our early recommendations was - you need to go out and you need to find the older women to match with them. And you can even see it on social media. An example that I love is a woman named Batty Winkle whose tagline is "stealing your

man since 1928", you know? She is phenomenal for showing all of us, not just young women, "You know what? I don't have to age like my grandmother did. I can still have an absolutely rockin life at 85."
And in fact, in terms of aspiration and the decisions I make right now, that has profound impact on what are my health choices, how do I dress, how do I speak, how do I move? What do I drink, the whole thing?
CG: Well, exactly what you and the alcohol industry have got to do is something that I've been talking about again for years, which is reinvent aspirational culture. And you kill several birds with one stone. Because when you create this campaign that features a range of old women, talking about how they manage their alcohol intake, you will impact younger women and men as well. I've been saying for years, the alcohol industry and every industry makes the enormous mistake of thinking that we older people aspire to be young. We don't. Younger people aspire to be us, because at this age we don't give a fuck about anything. We don't give a damn what anybody thinks. At this age, we've learned what really matters in relationships, in life. We have our own sense of personal style. We have our own sense of style. We have the freedom to travel to be who we want to be. We are starting businesses at the fastest rate of any age group. Younger people find all of that incredibly aspirational. What a total missed opportunity nobody is taking. When you do that, you kill several birds with one stone in terms of creating a huge social benefit for the alcohol industry.

The takeaway

"Marginalized groups have much to offer. Empower those who have been marginalized and communicate through demonstration."

Conversation XVI

EPISODE 970 - CHINEDU ROSA

The audio

The issues

This episode explores the opportunities and challenges facing the wine and hospitably sector in Nigeria from the perspective of successful female entrepreneur and how she creates non-judgmental spaces for cross-cultural culinary experiences.

The guest

A banker turned wine export consultant with over 22 years of experience in retailing and wholesale of fine wines in Lagos, Nigeria, her native country, Chinedu now runs her own consulting firm "Vines by Rosa" in Bordeaux, working with wine importers and exporters on both continents. She specializes in methodical wine selection, exporting, wine branding and marketing strategy tailored for Africa. She is founder and President of the Bordeaux Business Network and also President of Circle of Global Business Women.

The conversation

CR: My story is quite weird, not from a wine drinking family. I enjoyed wines because my uncle was an archbishop. He used to live in Rome and he would bring a couple of really lovely Tuscans back to Lagos. If you know Nigeria, it is actually a beer drinking country, and we love cold drinks, it's quite hot 34 degrees and above. People like refreshing drinks, so we come from a country of beer drinkers, but my dad wasn't a beer drinker, he wasn't really much of a drinker at all. But, you know, the heart wants what the heart wants. The first time I tasted a good bottle of wine, red wine, I was like, taken. This was when I was 16 and I was just like, oh my God, this is what I want to be drinking for the rest of my life. It was so nice. It was just delicious. Some people at the beginning, you either love it or you hate it. But for me, it was really instant love. I would tell my dad, "instead of beer, can we just get a bottle of wine? Can we? Whenever we travel, can somebody get us a bottle of wine?" I didn't even know a Merlot from a Cabernet Sauvignon. I didn't know any of that. I was just like beautiful wine, you know? And I'll be "yeah, it's so yummy. It's delicious."

PH: So, tell me a little bit about The Bordeaux Mentor Week and then I want to talk about how it came to be and how all of that experience of being an up-and-

coming Nigerian wine expert, all those years ago, has led to this moment.

CR: Well, honestly, I think the beauty about the partnership I have with Jane [Anson] is that we're so different but so alike. We talk differently. We appreciate things differently, but from the first day we sat down together, we looked at each other and said, "we're going to be friends". It was so funny. We have so many friends in common, but we got to talk seriously when she interviewed me about the first diversity in Bordeaux, and this she did for Decanter, and it was such a liberating experience for me to actually talk to somebody who was asking me the right questions. How do I feel here in Bordeaux? And then after that discussion, we looked at each other and she's like, "What are we going to do about this?" And I'm like, "Jane, I am doing my part. My part is to encourage more people to learn about wine, to host wine tastings." I do wine tastings in chateaux privately with guests, with Nigerian food. When I'm in Nigeria, I have been doing tastings since 2008 because after I was in Lebanon and my husband died, I moved back to Nigeria and I worked with his friends and we had the actual wine stores and that was my opportunity to really grow in the wine business.

The real thing that works with Nigeria - and this is why what I'm doing on Friday is so important for me - is actually tasting the wines with our local dishes.

When we bring new wines, we tell them, "Come try this, see if you like it." We're not even giving you, "Oh it is five years old. …" All the grammar and the BS that goes with, you know, trying to sell people what they don't need. For me, it's all about really finding what is your bliss in wine? What glass makes you say, "Mmmmm". What glass of wine makes you say, "I want to sit down with my wife and have a good chat"?

This is what this is. What is important is not you telling me what I should taste in the wine. You have the right to tell me what I should taste. I will decide what I'm tasting.

PH: A non-judgmental space?

CR: Non-judgmental. Nobody was trying to say, "Ooh, I smelled the blackcurrant here. Oh the blossom." Because seriously, we don't even have some of these smells. When I did my WSET courses, this was one of the first things I told my teacher. I said, "Listen, I am lucky and blessed enough to be somebody who has lived abroad, who has travelled. But come on, we don't even know most of the smells you're talking about. First of all, you guys need to expand your vocabulary. You need to expand your mindsets to encompass the world. I smell blond plantain in wines. I smell star fruit, the African star fruit, in wines and I can't explain it to you, so don't tell me what I'm tasting."

I know what I'm tasting. And all that matters is I like it or I don't. And this is why for my tastings, I actually taste up to three wines with one dish, and then you choose what suits you. You choose the one. I'm not telling you, you have to like this wine with this food, you're going to have a choice is going to be two, there's going to be three. And for each dish, you try each of this wine with that same dish, and you choose what is good for you, what you are comfortable with, what you say is yummy. I might say it's yucky and some of this is yummy, but I need to give you choices. You can't force people to put them in a box. This is this is one of the things that drive me crazy here. They want to put you in a frickin' box. You know, I refuse to be put in the box. You are not my maker, so you can't put me in a box.

PH: So, you've got the Bordeaux tastings that happen in Nigeria. But what I'm really curious about is, are you bringing that the other way?

CR: On Friday! This very Friday, I am hosting the second edition of the African Food and Wine Tasting in Bordeaux on the 17th. I did the first one in Paris, which was a huge hit. We had over 12 wines (minus the champagne) with ten dishes, and each of them were paired with 2-2-2. And then we did a twist and a shake up. … out of 50 people, there were 12 nationalities at the event. Twelve nationalities. More than half of them have never tasted Nigerian food before.

And it was an experience that for me it was so gratifying because this is what I do in Lagos. We started tasting [wine] with Nigerian dishes and people were now the elements that makes a wine yummy is the way you feel and the way you feel when you're eating. Your native dish is different from when you are being forced to eat salads across the chicken or whatever.

My spice is more delicious than anything else in the world as far as I'm concerned. No matter the kind of food you give me from wherever else you from what I am, I am is what is going to make me feel good.

PH: Yes. Okay. You're preparing these incredible African Nigerian dinners. So, I guess my first questions are, do you bring chefs and ingredients and everything over to make that authentic?

CR: Yeah! I will tell you something - I love cooking. First of all. So, all the ones I've been doing at the Chateaux, I made all the food. I bring my spices. I love cooking. I love feeding people, which is something my mom passed on to me. But for the dinners, because they are more than 40, I have a chef. I have one in Paris. I actually have three here in Bordeaux. And for this latest one, this is a secret, you're the first person I'm telling this, there's going to be Senegalese food and Nigerian food because I don't want it to just be a Nigerian experience. I want people to actually see the connection that Africa has to its food, to our taste. Because I don't sell wines only to Nigeria. I sell wines to Ghana, to Togo, Senegal, Cameroon. I want to expand the experience of everybody who comes in there. From the aperol, there are going to be snacks that we grew up on.

They're going to be so good that. What I want to know is how you enjoy your wine, what makes you tick, what gets into your head and makes you remember this glass of wine. Because, we forget, but actually, when you find that thing that really talks to you, you never forget the name of the wine. You never forget the region where the wines come from. I'm not cramming anything. I can't do that. It's too much luck. I would rather let a wine tell me how I feel. And then the wine becomes my lover.

The takeaway

"Create non-judgmental spaces and use language that reflects a diversity of backgrounds and cultural reference points."

Get U.S. Market Ready !!!

STEVE RAYE

Introduction

While it's the world's biggest political democracy, when it comes to wine, the U.S. is anything but. Post-prohibition legislation, the three-tier system, and the consolidation of distribution have combined to put obstacles in place that effectively prevent consumers from "voting" with their wallets.

So, the American market has developed an ever-expanding range of workarounds that allow producers to navigate entry to what we like to call a "complex market". And that market is changing. Recently, there has been significant growth in the numbers of small and mid-sized importers open to and exploiting niche opportunities.

Add to the "uniqueness" of the American market the existence of 52 different regulatory entities, each with their own rules, requirements and vocabulary.

So, then, where does Democracy fit in regard to wine?

Democracy is defined as a form of governmental supreme power vested in the people, who exercise direct or indirect control through a system of free elections. In contrast to that noble ideal, the wine and spirit business is regulated and controlled through state liquor control departments run by appointed officials. The regulations on which that control is based were put in place back in 1933 to avoid the problems that caused Prohibition in the first place, and those that evolved in the period between 1920 and 1933. We live in a very different commercial environment now, and the result is something that is far from the Democratic Ideal.

So, I've taken the point of view that Democracy in Wine speaks to equal access of consumers to products imported into and sold within the US, a subject is fundamental to the focus of my book, *How to Get U.S. Market-Ready* and my consulting working with brands to help them navigate the complexities of the U.S. market.

Bottom line, it's not easy. But it is possible. The best advice I can give is not to repeat the same mistakes everyone else has made in the past.

The interviews that follow have been selected and edited to showcase those questions that relate to US market access.

Conversation XVII

EPISODE 514 – CHERYL DURZY

The audio

The issues

The three-tier system of alcohol distribution is the system for distributing alcoholic beverages set up in the United States after the repeal of Prohibition. The three tiers are (i) importers or producers; (ii) distributors; and (iii) retailers. Producers can only sell their products to wholesale distributors who then sell to retailers. Only retailers can sell to consumers. In other words, producers cannot sell directly to the consumer export producers cannot sell directly to the consumer (domestic winery sales direct to consumer are one of those maddening "wrinkles" in the American system). In some American states, part or all of the distribution tier, and sometimes also the retail tier, are operated by the state itself (or by contractors operating on behalf of the state), rather than by private commercial entities. This episode explores how technology, and the internet in particular, are providing various solutions to the challenges posed by the three-tier system, enabling producers to establish a more direct relationship with their customers.

The guest

Cheryl Murphy Durzy managed wholesale sales for her family's 80,000 case winery, Clos LaChance, for over 17 years. In June 2016, she started LibDib, the first alcohol distributor and technology company to offer a three-tier compliant web-based platform. She sits on several boards including the California Sustainable Wine Association and Free the Grapes.

The conversation

CD: I was really struggling to sell my cases of wine that I was allocated to sell every year, and it was because I was losing distributors left and right. They were either getting bought out, they weren't paying me, there were all kinds of challenges for us as a small to mid-size winery. Being here in Silicon Valley I said, hey, there's got to be a technology way or a marketplace that we can create that will allow for three-tier distribution for all wineries and all distilleries who need distribution. That was the start of the company, and we've evolved over time. We've been doing this almost four years, now. We're currently in six states, and any winery and any distillery can get online and have distribution in a matter of sometimes days and at the most, a couple of weeks. It's the most efficient path to market, and it's definitely the least expensive when it comes to getting into the distribution world.

SR: How does LibDib differ from the traditional three-tier system or is it functioning within the three-tier system but with emphasis in different places?

CD: Yes, absolutely. It is important to note that we are part of a three-tier system. We are a licensed wholesaler in the states that we operate in. That's an important piece of the puzzle. We pay taxes, we follow all the compliance rules, we're certainly not trying to disrupt or break anything when it comes to the three-tier system. We operate within the system and that's how we built our platform. We differ in that we are really a technology platform. We're a marketplace, and any supplier can be a part of it. That's very different than the traditional distribution model where you have to pitch a distributor, they have to decide if they're going to take you on, you have to negotiate margins, you have to launch the product, you've got to work with their salesforce. We've actually built the platform so that the maker themselves can be that salesforce. I was in sales, I worked with my distributors, but there was really no better salesperson than me versus my distributor sales rep to pitch my products. So, I was able to be a lot more efficient in the marketplace, and that's how we built the platform. The shipping model is different in that we don't take pallets and store them in warehouses and ship them after a sales rep sells them. It actually is a just-in-time shipping model. We get a demand for an order, we order the product, we get it on the road in a number of different ways, whatever is compliant in that market, and then it's delivered to the account at some point. So, it's just very different.

SR: A lot of the people listening here, are interested in the US of course, but the focus is on Italy, and there's another layer in the chain there with an importer. Can you talk about how imported brands differ from domestic brands that are using the LibDib

platform?
CD: Sure. We purchase from an importer, so any winery or distillery from Europe needs to be working with an importer in order to work with LibDib, because we have to purchase from a US entity that has what's called a "Basic Permit". Once you're with an importer and in the United States, you can be in any of the LibDib markets. That import piece is key. We can't work with someone without an importer.
SR: So, a supplier who is interested in using you has to come to the party with an import solution, and I'm sure there's a variety of those. Can you speak to that?
CD: Oh, there's all kinds. There's a number of different types of importers. But here's something that I'm super interested in, and this ties into our whole e-commerce thing, is how can a lot, and I've been talking to a lot of wineries from all over the world, all they really want when they get to the US is a direct-to-consumer presence. How can they do that through the three-tier system? An importer can't sell direct-to-consumer. They still have to go through a distributor and a retailer. It's been fascinating starting to work with some of these different companies that can provide this e-commerce marketplace for, I like to call it e-premise, you have on-premise, off-premise, e-premise, they can provide these online marketplaces for direct-to-consumer and via the importer and LibDib and some of these programs for the winery wouldn't have to deal with kind of the traditional model, which takes so long and so much money, as you know.
SR: The internet and the various ways of getting to the

consumer have changed how wine is being marketed in the US. Can you comment on that?

CD: Absolutely. Things have really changed, I've noticed, with domestic and out-of-the-country suppliers, when it comes to managing your brand and how your brand is built online. There's so much money being put into various marketing programs, and the greatest thing about that is if that's kind of your path to market, you can measure it, right? So you can know if I put in X amount of dollars into this marketing channel online and I'm going through these direct-to-consumer channels, I know how much my customer acquisition cost is and what my customer lifecycle is and all of those things that have been so hard to measure in the past when it comes to the three-tier system, because you work two or three tiers separated from your end customer. A lot of wineries especially in Europe are used to this because you can do this in Europe and you can ship direct-to-consumer, your distributors can ship direct-to-consumer, it's a lot different than it is here. But now with a lot of these different programs in place, the wineries can now have that direct relationship with their customers, which I think is the future of alcohol and e-commerce alcohol. It's going to be how you connect with your consumer, remarket to them, how are you selling to them and how are you finding them? What are you spending to find those people or how are they finding you? Hopefully when the world opens up again after COVID, there's going to be a lot of travel and people will be going back into the world and going to visit wineries. How can they continue to get those bottles from their favorite winery in Italy, right? That is now going to be possible when people invest in these different channels here in the US.

SR: You can now have a direct communication with the people who are buying your product in spite of or using the three-tier system and maintain the relationship with the customer without having to rely on the retailer to do that. That's great, except for, now what do the retailers do?

CD: Exactly. And you lose a lot. Through some of the programs that we're seeing is the retailers are just fulfillment houses, for the most part. This is important when you're deciding on and these types of programs, they started with distilleries, but I'm starting to see more and more importers working with these programs. If you send someone to a retailer, you don't know what happens at that point, right? They can go anywhere, and they can click on something else, or maybe they buy something, maybe they don't. But with some of these programs, you know exactly what they bought, and you know exactly how to get back in touch with them. You have all their contact information, which I think invaluable when it's building a brand here.

SR: The challenge for a lot of wineries, in many cases, who are just farmers, that's their principal business, don't have the experience or expertise or time to learn all that. How do you onboard people so that they can have a graphic dashboard so they can see what's going on?

CD: Well, the whole point of a dashboard is to make something really easy to read, right? With graphs and to say, okay, whatever insight you're looking into, you want to be able to know exactly what you're looking at with the dashboard. But I 100% agree with you that it has to be turned into actions. There's a lot of opportunity there where you can say, okay, it looks like this is happening with Nebbiolo, for example, in this part of the country. How can you literally break that down and say, contact this buyer? Because that's what it means, right? It all comes down to how to sell a case and how to get that placement and how to build that relationship and translates into dollars. That's going to be the next step, how do you take these insights and then recommend actions and have people follow through on those actions?

The most successful brands that we've seen, international brands, to be honest, have some kind of sales representation in the United States. Otherwise it's just too hard to do it, right? I've done it the other way. When I was selling wine for my family's winery, I was also working in Europe, and just going to Europe twice a year was not enough, first of all, to try and build a presence. It was very time consuming to do it, too. If you're really going to commit to the United States now, this could be different if you're just focusing on the direct-to-consumer channel, right? But if you're going to commit to the United States and you want to get into restaurants or if you have a plan, what's your plan and your plan is outside of kind of that channel, then you really should have someone here helping you. There's lots of different companies that can provide that feet-on-the-street access. But as I mentioned before, it's really interesting what brands can do now, just direct-to-consumer if they invest in it. So, if you have a good story or if you have a customer list for people that visited your winery, how can you potentially take advantage of that and build on that over time?

SR: How does LibDib fit into the on-premise world?

CD: We sell to hundreds and thousands of restaurants and bars and hotels and boats. We have a category on there for boats that have bars on them. I would say on-premise for the last year has been nothing, right? We went from being about 35% on-premise last March, and it went down to pretty much zero. It's starting to come back, which is cool. New York just opened up 25% post- COVID, and we're starting to see the bars reordering. We were pretty tied in with a lot of the very crafty, cool cocktail bars, especially in New York and LA on the restaurant side.

We started building some really good relationship with sommeliers, especially in New York, because they're always looking for something that's unique and different and we have thousands of wines on the platform. But as I said, it just went to nothing at the end of last March. It's going to be really interesting, this whole reopening, because a lot of people sold off their cellars to stay afloat. I don't think there's going to be a huge capital investment in wine cellars. People are going to have less things on the list, but they still have to find that selection for people. It's going to be really interesting what happens post-Covid. There's a lot of opportunity in getting on these lists and building these relationships with these sommeliers and the buyers. The cool thing about LibDib is you can offer those types of things that they want when it comes to, you know, can you offer a mixed case where it's four bottles of Cab, four bottles of Pinot, and four bottles of Pinot Grigio so that someone doesn't have to commit to three cases, you're keeping an eye on their capital expenditures as well. That's not super easy to do with a traditional distributor, but it's very easy to do with LibDib.

SR: We've seen a shrinking of inventory, as you alluded to, but also in terms of what they think is the sweet spot going forward. So, if they had 60 wines on the list before COVID, they might be looking for a target of 30 now. During this period, it's been reverting to those brands that are familiar. LibDib is almost the opposite of that, I would imagine, its mostly brands that people are not familiar with.

CD: Yes. That's been very interesting because especially at the grocery channel people have been looking for the familiar because they don't want to walk in and spend hours at the grocery store looking for stuff. They want to get in and get out. Where we've really seen our business grow since the pandemic, was online with a lot of our e-premise and a lot of our retailers, because people are spending the time online and shopping and looking for new things and researching and all of that, whereas it definitely wasn't happening at the chain level, which is interesting because at the beginning of last year, beginning of 2020, I actually launched a chain department because you can't sell. Selling to the chains is very different than just selling to a restaurant, right. Or having a buyer go online and source something. The chains don't do that. You have to get on a presentation schedule, and you got to go in and send a sample. There's a whole process to it.

SR: Are you working with any Italian wines now?

CD: Currently, we don't have any Italian wineries that are doing any significant business. But we have a ton signed up on the platform and figuring it out. What are they going to do? When are they going to invest? I've had some great conversations with some people lately who are building businesses around this kind of direct-to-consumer model for imports. It'll be interesting to see what happens over the next six to twelve months when it comes to importing wines. The whole tariff situation has made things really hard.

SR: I tell people working in the United States, it's like peeling an onion. Every time you peel a layer, there's another layer underneath and it makes you cry.

CD: I read that in your book. It's true! Even if you're domestic, it makes you cry.

Once you figure it out, it's all about the relationship with the customer, whether it comes to the consumer or that trade customer. Look at the big suppliers here in the US, what are they doing? They've got their own salespeople out there building their own relationships. People have to invest in sales and marketing of their brand, whether it's the direct-to-consumer side, whether it's building the relationships with the restaurants, whether it's getting into the cocktail bars. You have to figure out what's your path to market and what are you going to invest in it, because if you don't invest in it, it's just like posting and praying. You can throw something up on the internet and hope that someone buys something, but that's not how you build a business. You've got to go out and you got to sell.

That's the most successful suppliers on our platform who are out there and have the plan of how they're going to get to market and what are they going to do. Those are the ones that are the most successful on traditional distribution as well.

SR: So, when we talk about take responsibility for your brand and all that, when we talk about online premise, what are some of the components that are mission critical?

CD: You need to have a good story. You still have to have all of those things that you need when you're launching a brand. What's your story, what are your images? Have beautiful images. Make sure your branding is consistent. Have a good brand voice. Differentiate yourself from competition. The wine and spirits industry is heavily, heavily competitive in terms of how many players there are out there. But if you make sure that you're doing all of those things and then have an easy way for customers to find you, make sure you have your social media with all your links. You'd be surprised, so many people have a website and there's no link on where they can buy something. That's step one of 100. You should always tell people where they can buy something and have a Buy It Now button and all of those types of things.

My goal was to help the three-tier system to evolve with the times and with technology, and I believe we're well on our way. Ten to fifteen years ago nobody thought that anybody would buy clothes online, and now look at clothes and shoes. There's so much headway. There are so many things that are going to happen in the next five to ten years and just everybody should have their plan. Have your online plan.

The takeaway

"Embrace new technology that has opened up direct-to-consumer channels that allow producers to manage and build their brand online."

Conversation XVIII

EPISODE 539 – NICOLE BRASSARD JORDAN

The audio

The issues

Alcoholic beverage control states, generally known as control states, are 17 states in the United States that have state monopoly over the wholesaling or retailing of some or all categories of alcoholic beverages (including beer, wine, and distilled spirits). This episode explores how one of those control states operates in practice

The guest

Nicole Brassard Jordan is a 30-year industry veteran and Deputy Commissioner of the New Hampshire Liquor Commission. In her role, Jordan is responsible for conceptualizing and implementing industry-leading strategies to increase sales throughout the state's 67 NH Liquor & Wine Outlet locations and off-premise channels. She previously was the first female to serve as Director of Sales, Marketing, Merchandising, and Warehousing and still oversees those areas of the business.

The conversation

SR: Let's talk about the Liquor Commission and give us an overview of the philosophy of why it exists and how it stands out in the scheme of all the other control states.

NB: Okay. Well, listeners may or may not know that there are 17 control states left in the U.S. from prohibition, New Hampshire being one of them. We have a couple of others surrounding us, Vermont as well as Maine. These are where alcohol sales are managed by the individual states. New Hampshire has 69 outlets that we operate throughout the state. Our philosophy is really simple: we want consumers to have an outstanding shopping experience, great selection and outstanding savings, which is why we call it an outlet. We service about 12 million customers annually, and last fiscal year we ended at about $750 million in sales. We expect to eclipse that this year with just under $800 million.

SR: I think that's really significant. The size of it is not astonishing, but it's significant. For a lot of people not

from the US, they're thinking about grocery chains or chains like Total Wine and so forth, but the control states in many cases dwarf those.

NB: They do, and I say it because I work for the New Hampshire Liquor Commission and I'm part of it, but we are the number one control state in my mind, and a lot of other control states look to us for best practices and visit New Hampshire to get some ideas on how they can enhance their stores or have better communication with their customers. They've been to many of our events. We offer several things, some best practices for other controlled states

SR: When I think about control states, one of the key benefits I stress to clients that I consult with is the consistency in execution that you can get from a control state that you cannot get in an open state. If you do a deal with control states that have X number of displays or this kind of promotional support or particular shelf positioning, it's pretty much guaranteed that it will get executed exactly and in full. There's no way you can make that happen in the open states, you're reliant on the distributor and the individual retail stores. Take New York, that's really difficult to do.

NB: That's correct. They're basically knocking door to door, and when they come to us, we're talking about 69 locations throughout the state. So, yes, we execute products really well. It's very clear, we partner with our suppliers and wineries and distilleries that want to work with us. We have many opportunities for their brands to be successful, but it's a partnership, and we really look at it that way.

SR: That's very refreshing. I'm not going to say it's rare, but we don't often hear that much in open states simply because there's no one person in charge. If you're just talking to the state liquor authority, they're usually lawyers trying to tell you that you can't do whatever it is you're calling to ask, can I do this? At least that's been my experience. One of the issues of retail stores in general is the ability to staff it with people who are knowledgeable enough to help the consumer ask questions, answer questions, and learn things, and then the role of in-store, point-of-sale, shelf talkers, case cards, and those kinds of things. If your goal is to work collaboratively with the producer to make a better experience for the consumer, what kind of support do you guys rely on to extend what the individual people in the stores can provide?

NB: All those key things that you had mentioned are very important, and we do educational training, we have a designated educator in wine, and he also does spirits for our staff in the stores. That is a big component of that. We do a number of events throughout the year. We have a spirits week that's designated in November. We also have a wine week, which is designated in January. Those have been going on for many years. Our staff go to those events to learn and meet the producers themselves. That's what we pride ourselves on, is to have a lot of those producers come to those events so that they can talk not only with our staff, but also the consumers that purchase their products. So, they're building brand ambassadors within the state, or let's just say there's probably an awful lot of people from

Massachusetts, and as you are from Connecticut coming up to these events, that also spread the word when you go home that you've met them and you've tried their wines and you're really excited about them, and you tell all your friends, which is a great position for producers to be in, to be able to talk to them and tell them the stories, because that's so important when it comes to really reaching consumers. We've got great relationships with many producers in Italy, and they are ambassadors and want to come here every single year for our events for that reason. They want to talk to those consumers, and they see results, that's the other part of this. Those events really do show results for these producers, and consumers show that they're purchasing those products right through and well after those events.

SR: That raises a question: what level of data is accessible by suppliers?

NB: We supply all of the data to the broker who is in state that works on behalf of the supplier. We have a broker community, and it's very important. The reason that I say that is we're running a wholesale business as well as a retail business. You need to have people on the streets for these specific brands, which is why they work with local brokers. They'll go to the restaurants; they will do events at restaurants. They will also bring point-of-sale materials to U.S. and other off-premise accounts that sell those products. So, it's very important to have that broker community and those boots on the street regarding those various suppliers and producers.

SR: Thinking about Italy again, give us an example of

some things that you guys have brought in. I realize you're not a buyer anymore, but you're certainly aware of what's coming in, that represent trends for Italian wines in the US. We know about Prosecco and some of those things but talk a little bit about that.

NB: Yes, certainly Prosecco has definitely taken off. We've seen that for a number of years. Lambrusco has come in. It's still a very small category, but people are starting to warm up to it. It's really funny, because when it comes to Italian wines, I'm just going to go back to a producer that we worked with and we actually wrote a label for, because we said to him, you have really great wines and we want New Hampshire consumers to try an entry level wine with the varietal on the front of the label, and we wanted to say Sangiovese and lo and behold…we had a producer and we wrote the back label copy so that it was what do you pair it with and all those things and where it was from. In this particular case, to put Sangiovese on the front label, it was off the charts, it was off the charts. New Hampshire was the beta test for it, and now he's selling it throughout the United States. It's just something that Italian producers may not appreciate that the U.S. market doesn't understand the village or the town concept. We understand that you have to know those things and you have to know the varietals within those areas, but in this particular case we wanted to show consumers that here's the variety and it's right there and you can't miss it. And by the way, this is by a producer that you really know, and you've purchased their wines and you can really enjoy this wine out by the campfire, having pizza, out by the barbecue…

SR: There's the on-premise, there's the off-premise, and now everyone's talking about the e-premise. Can you talk about how you guys are getting involved in that? That incorporates not only e-commerce itself, but also the concepts of in-store, curbside pickup and where in New Hampshire is and where you guys are going?

NB: Well, of course, the onset of COVID made us accelerate the things that we were working on. We put a curbside and in-store pick up in place in the spring of 2020 to help consumers. At the same time, we've been working on a whole new POS system and also a website. We launched the new website in September, which also included our curbside and in-store pick up, but you purchase online, you pay for it online, which is not something we could do with the old system. When we went live with the curbside and in-store pick up in the spring, people couldn't pay for it online. They actually paid for it when they arrived at the store, at their car, on the curbside, or they came into the store and purchased it at that time. Now we've transitioned. We now have 15 stores that are up and running with curbside and in store pick up. You go on our website, and you can purchase the products. Consumers will go to one of those stores to pick it up either curbside or in store. Since we launched that new online purchasing, we've done 1.5 million in a very short period of time and done over 8000 various orders, so we're very excited about that opportunity. We think it's the way of the future. The next thing that we're going to be doing, we're hoping to launch in the spring of 2021, will be in state delivery. So yes, we're fast-tracking things.

SR: To a degree, the experience of many producers from outside the U.S. is it's just a function of price and how low can you go? It sounds like you guys have more holistic perspective on that, that is more than just buying cheap.

NB: Yes. In the end, the consumer is going to dictate what they're going to pay for our product, and our partnership has to get US to the fair price and when we're going to put those items on sale and regular programming so that consumers can see that we're willing to put some money behind these brands. There is an approach where you have to all work together, whether it be the POS, we'll need ratings, we'll need all of those things that help sell wine. Of course, the story is right behind them. The other thing that COVID made us do as a retailer is that we had to pivot a lot of these events to online and social media. We were doing a lot of Facebook lives - a lot, I mean on a weekly basis. We replaced our major events, the two that I talked about, Spirits Week and Wine Week, with 90 days around the world. It was meant to bring the consumers and the producers together to taste and talk about wine together. We would give them a list of wines that will be talked about, and then they could purchase them prior to their Facebook live. They'd sign up to be able to go to that. Then, of course, we gave them some discounts on those wines after they participated. It is a partnership and we're all going to give a little, but we all need to make money. At some point we have to decide, is this product going to make it or is it not going to make it? What are we going to do to help it make it? Then we just have those conversations about what's next? Where do we go?

SR: I see there's a couple of stores that I know that

have extremely capable writers who are posting three or four times a week, long-form, and reaching many thousands of buyers. These are people who buy pretty much not exclusively, but specifically from that particular store. So, in terms of the power of communications, getting involved and associated with a major retailer, like the New Hampshire Liquor Commission, is a win-win for everybody.

NB: Sure is. We have a very experienced wine writer on our staff as well. He's the educator, of course, so he's putting out an awful lot of information on our behalf, and our store folks love it, but also the consumers love it. He had a column in one of our publications that we've done away with and replaced with something else, but he had a fan following like you wouldn't believe.

SR: We're coming to the end of our time allotment, but one of the questions I want to ask is the big takeaway.

NB: I think people just need to know that we're open. We're open to have conversations, to look at the products that are being offered, determine whether or not it's viable in our system and understand what type of opportunities they have to help us sell these products. The partnership is really the most important part that we are willing to have, and we're not closed minded. We're not going to just say this is the number, this is the number without talking about how we think it would best go to market in our market.

The takeaway

"Foster partnerships with relevant stakeholders to understand and gain access to complex liquor markets."

Conversation XIX

EPISODE 639 – GARY FISCH

The audio

The issue

Retailer's perspective on the U.S. market.

The guest

Gary Fisch is an industry-leading retailer in the New Jersey market with four stores in operation, two owned by him and two by his wife. He has also recently opened a new store in the former Dean and Deluca space in the Napa Valley.

The conversation

SR: Gary, can you give us a short profile of when you first got into the industry, some of the stores that you started, and how you got to where you are in Napa now?

GF: We opened our first store in Madison, New Jersey in 1987. It was a 1200 square foot store doing about

$700,000 a year. It was designed to be a part-time job, which became a lifetime passion. We moved that store a couple of times and in 1994 we ended up in our 13,000 square foot location in Madison. Since then, we've opened stores up around New Jersey.

SR: You're deep in Italian wines in many of your stores. Talk about the trends that you're seeing in terms of whatever you want to talk about, in terms of varietals, regions, pricing, or even variances and preferences by store, at least between the ones in New Jersey and California is probably domestic.

GF: It's funny. When we talked about doing this podcast, I went to Cesare Martini [Gary's Italian wine buyer] for the Italian part, but he's actually in Italy for the next three weeks. I know we had a business plan meeting plan there, but I think with them and soccer, I think he extended how long he's going to be there. As I said, I let Cesare do everything Italian, but because of that, I believe we have by far the best Italian selection in New Jersey and one of the best in the country, considering we're a store that has great product from around the world. Italian, even though I would say we're domestically focused, Italian wines for us represents between ten and 13% of our total business, which is very strong. The hot category, we're obviously very strong in Tuscany and Piedmont, Cesare is a northern Italian gentleman, and clearly that's his strength, but we're also rapidly growing our Sicilian portfolio and our southern Italy portfolio, as well as non-Pinot Grigio whites. We're in New Jersey, right? Cavit Pinot Grigio is the king of Italian white, and it still is around the country, and it is definitely in our stores, but we're finding some great Vernaccias and Vermentinos and other spectacular higher acidity, fresh flavorful Italian whites that we can introduce people to. That has been our mantra for everything is finding wines we can introduce people to. Cesare, with his family connections and his personal connections, has been able to keep is in front of the curve and keep us really growing in the right direction and discontinuing items that don't sell or aren't selling fast enough to replace them with what's hot and what's going on.

SR: Do you see Americans becoming more aware or interested in Italian wines? Do they recognize the incredible range of indigenous varietals that are there?

GF: We've always done a lot of Italian business. To understand Italy is to understand the food, right. Having great Italian restaurants, I've always said if you want to drink great wine, you drink it from the place of origin. You eat the same food. It seems to work, and they've done it.

SR: If it grows together, it goes together.

GF: Is the American public embracing Italy? I would say absolutely, but we're ahead of that. I couldn't speak to Dallas, Texas, if they sell as much Italian wine as we do. But having said that, it's definitely growing beyond Chianti and Brunello di Montalcino, where Piedmont is really on fire for US. You mentioned Taurasi, Mastroberardino. That whole area has some great lines. I said Sicily because I think that they're on fire and the price points are great. It's almost like the further from Germany and northern Italy, the lower the prices are. So, if you can't drive there, it's less expensive. It's a great way to get value.

SR: Recently there's been a major shift towards e-commerce, not just in the wine industry, but all over, but it's been dramatic in wines, and spirits for that matter. Your site, which is a very active e-commerce site, the back end is run by City Hive, and I know the guys, Roi Kliper and Haim Chasman, who had developed that. Tell me about how that's working for you, and particularly the e-commerce piece of that.

GF: We're very fortunate. My son, as he was finishing his MBA, came to work with us. Part of his first real job was to help figure out e-commerce platforms for us. He interviewed three or four people that had mobile devices, websites, and he picked City Hive. He thought that they were by far light years ahead of everybody, that they had great ownership and management structure. So, we went with them probably two years before the pandemic. So, we had our mobile site up and running, but not active. On 1 March 2020, we probably had 1500 mobile users. Now we have over 30,000 mobile users. When the pandemic hit us hard, we decided on 20 March, our stores were like Christmas, it was a zoo in all of our stores, we decided to close.

Even though we were legally allowed to stay open, I just felt for the health and safety of our teams that we needed to close. So, we closed, literally. We were open on the 20th. I said to Mike, and he was staying at our house, I turned to him, and I said, can we succeed if we're closed? And he said, he'll work with Roi, and we'll make it happen. So, we shut the doors, we put up signs in the stores and sent out emails and social media saying we're only open for curbside pickup or local delivery. We went from 99% retail to 100% not retail. I got to tell you, the first two weeks were hairy to say the least, switching, ramping up the stores. City Hive, our mobile app, was not designed for that kind of volume. We were running on parallel tracks because it had to then talk to our website, which was a separate website, so you could buy it on our website and buy it on the mobile app, and it was drawing from the same inventory. So, we had inventory issues. Michael converted US, our website to City Hive, in the middle of all this, which allowed us to save that step and cause it to be smoother. We bought more trucks, we rented trucks. We hired, I think, 80 people. We went to shifts, so that we would have people come in at five in the morning, and then another crew come in late to stay till about midnight so that we could pull and get all the orders ready to go for pickup or delivery. We're very fortunate because the technology was there to allow for us to do what we needed to do.

SR: There are some 650 indigenous varietals in Italy, and I've heard 175,000 individual producers. Very few of them are here. Everybody wants to be here. It's a challenge, especially with distributor consolidation and all the limitations on intra and interstate e-commerce, less over wines than for spirits. But still, in all, I look at stores like yours and tools like City Hive, and there are others. We're doing some testing with a number of these players. I see a lot of opportunities or potential opportunities for individual suppliers to leverage tools such as City Hive to communicate directly with retailers, not bypassing the three-tier system at all, but at least main-

taining some level of control that isn't interrupted by the noise or the friction at the importer and the wholesale level. Can you comment on that?

GF: You bring up a great point. With City Hive we don't bypass the wholesaler, right. But again, to go back to the Drizly model, the wholesalers or the suppliers are paying Drizly to advertise their brands, and those are big brands, right? You're not seeing that little boutique Brunello or Sicilian red advertised under his, you're seeing Cupcake and Santa Margarita and Josh Cellars and Jose Cuervo or whatever being advertised. With City Hive, we're able to work with smaller producers and feature them and then buy them through the three-tier, however we end up doing it and putting great content on. We're working on doing more videos. Some of these smaller wineries, we will have a video with them. So, it definitely allows us to work well with City Hive as well as the producer to provide our consumer great product and a way to get it and learn about it in a way that we still control their information, and we can direct to them. If we know they're buying Pinot Grigios and we have a program on an Italian white that we love, we could target them directly so that they're seeing what they want to say, learning about what they want to learn.

It's still a challenge, right, because they have to get it here. My pie-in-the sky solution would be this 5000-case producer in the Veneto would bring 100 cases or 200 cases into the country through some importer. They would assign a wholesale partner that doesn't take a big fee, because some of the big wholesalers mark it up 30-40%, they take good markups. What we would do with them is we would promote their items and buy as needed and maybe the City Hive network will all buy those products.

We have a partnership. The way I look at it is it's not an economic partnership, it's a partnership.

SR: It's a commercial partnership. You guys make each other's businesses better.

GF: It's a commercial partnership with City Hive. When we have an issue, we talk to Roi. If Roi can't solve it, he finds somebody on this team that can solve it. Trust me, my son is constantly looking to improve our systems, and so it's using technology and the information we get from that to better serve our clients. The better we serve our clients, the more they want to do with us, the more we want to do with us, the more information comes through City Hive, the more information that the supplier partners that we work with can find the basket size. What else goes in that basket? Did the people that buy my Pinot Grigio, did they also buy an Italian red wine? Did they buy prosciutto from you? What else did they buy? As we build this network, normally I would want to be exclusive. I'd want to be the only store that has City Hive, but that's not to my advantage, to be honest with you.

The takeaway

> **"New technology can allow smaller producers to engage directly with consumers in a meaningful and profitable way."**

Conversation XX

EPISODE 644 – JOSH WAND

The audio

The issues

How hiring has fundamentally changed in America, and not just solely due to COVID-19.

The guest

Josh Wand is the Founder & Motivator in Chief of Bev-Force, a boutique recruiting and staffing agency that specializes in hiring strategies and organizational design for beverage companies, nationwide.

The conversation

JW: My advice to anyone is if you want to build your own business or you want to create your own business, do it while you have a job, do it at night, do it on the weekends. Like make sure that when you can jump off, you're fully into it, put the plan in place first. So, I put the plan in place while I was still doing a rum thing on the nights, on the weekends. It turns out that guys that I was working with, the rum business, are very dear friends to this day. I'm actually going to one of their bachelor parties this weekend. I just got to a point where I said, all right, this is fully baked. I think I can do it. So, we launched in 2007, BevForce, which was basically affirmed to help companies find leaders and grow talent. But we said we want to have a tech-enabled platform. We want to build a marketplace, and we want to have high touch handheld white glove service too, so we can help build orders. So, we did it. We launched in 2007. It's morphed into multiple entities that now consist of BevForce, which was beverage - alcohol, which is our primary focal point, which is where we were born. But we do nonalcoholic beverages, sparkling waters, juices, sodas, all the stuff you can buy in a Whole Foods. We also launched another division called Food Force, then we have Beauty Force, and we have Herb Force, which is in the cannabis space, which we're pretty deep in, and Pet Force. So, it's all about consumer, consumer tech brands and beverage alcohol, wine, spirits, beer. It's something I'm really passionate about. We get to help a lot of great people find their dream jobs and help companies find great people to bring their mission to life. So, it's pretty fulfilling.

SR: We're coming out of COVID and all that. What's the future of the office in America? In a post-COVID world of remote work and Zoom meetings, we've seen some dramatic changes in the world take place. We're still not out of COVID by a long shot, but a whole lot of things have changed. Give us your perspective on it from the hiring entities.

JW: A big part of what we do is organizational design and advisory work, to think about the future state of the industry and these companies that are looking, they have to change the structure and their makeup and how they've operated, because no longer are the days of all employees must report to central headquarters and go there five days a week. I believe those days are numbered. Five days a week in an office, unless it's a production facility or essential work, it's very challenging to attract people to that. I believe there's going to be a hybrid situation, and we're already seeing it. Linkedin just announced a couple of days ago that in perpetuity, their teams can work remotely. It's so interesting where, backtrack two years ago, because I was an office person, we had a wonderful treehouse in the sky in Tribeca, fed people and had games and cultural activities and all this amazing connectivity. It was wonderful. Literally, it drove me. It was one of the things I loved most about the business. But people always wanted to have the optionality to work remote, and I was opposed to it. I was like, I don't know, I don't know if we'll get the output, will you really be connected? Like, really, you should be here, right?

SR: Old school management questions about how is this really going to work? Well, now we know it works, but how does it work?

JW: Well, I questioned it. I am a huge proponent of it now. We have people working in 15/16 states across the country have decided they can live wherever they want to live. Right now, we're approaching a situation where we realize the importance of giving access and freedom for people to be wherever they want to be. You can find the best people anywhere if you let them live anywhere. So, the talent pool has opened up pretty significantly because it's not just about finding people in New York or LA or Chicago, you can find them anywhere. However, people miss people and people want to be around people. It's very challenging to work in a silo in a 500 square foot apartment in the Lower East Side of New York when it's freezing cold, you want to go to an office, you want to have coffee, you want to see people. These are where a lot of your relationships exist. We were spending more time with our team members than we were our family. Well, the pendulum shifted where people have more of their own private time now and more of their alone time and less time commuting. However, they want to be able to see people. So, we're going to be doing a lot of leadership retreats. We're going to be doing combination in different markets where people can come in a couple of days a week and work together in spaces, but for impactful meetings, not administrative work, where I'm sitting shoulder to shoulder typing and logging my conversations in Salesforce. But the type of meetings that require strategic collaboration. The big thing that gets missed with the virtual workforce is after the meeting, tapping someone on the shoulder and saying, hey, here's what I meant by that. You want to go grab a coffee? Did you get that? Did you understand what that meant? Because I'm here to support you. I want to mentor you. For someone that's out of college, who's never worked in office environment, it is so hard to learn on Zoom.

SR: How does that work?

JW: Mentorship programs. We're working with several companies on this really developing tracks within organizations and allowing people that are early in their career, they might be looking to work in new functions of the business, to connect directly with someone who's a thought leader in that space and kind of bring them under their wing. And whether that's virtually or grabbing a virtual coffee once a week or a real coffee if they happen to be in the same market or getting together once a month, like real accountability. I believe that now more than ever leadership coaching is critical. Coaching for C suite, coaching for VPs, directors, managers, early stage. We have a whole leadership coaching band across the organization for all of the emerging thought leaders in our company because it's so important. They want to work on growth, and it's really hard to do that independently. What I would say is office space is definitely back. It's coming back. Delta is throwing everyone for loop. People will be in offices again, for sure. But when they're not required to be there five days a week, will they live in the most expensive cities in America?

SR: That's the question. What is the purpose of the city now when proximity and centrality were kind of core? And now what is New York going to do to survive this?

JW: I think not only will we survive, but we might also just thrive. You talk to people that have space and the quality of work that they can. Now listen, not all work can be done independently. Retail work can't be done independently. You got to go into retail. If you're in production and you're in wine making, in distillation, you got to be there. But for the professional services side of it, sales, marketing, finance, operations, D&C, e-commerce? People want flexibility. And now more than ever, the beverage alcohol industry is going through this transformation of direct-to-consumer and online. And where are they attracting people from? Beauty, personal care, consumer products, luxury lifestyle, Instagram brands, all the stuff that we buy every day. It's all happening in beverage alcohol. Where do these people live? Not in all of the major markets where all the beverage alcohol companies are the best people, are the best people. Being flexible in where they live will enable companies and organizations to attract the best and brightest talent for their specific organ. Everyone's got their own different culture, however, setting expectations and letting people know you might be working remote, but this is how often we're getting together, and this is how it's going to work. If you're not going to spend the money on the office space, you got to spend the money on bringing people together for experiences.

SR: Our industry, and maybe it's because I also fall into this category, tends to be old white men who have been there for their whole professional life. Is that changing?

JW: It has to change. It has to change. If the industry wants to continue to prosper, if we want to continue to lead the charge, there is zero question. I was just having a talk with Deborah Brenner from Women of the Vine and Spirits. Last week we did a LinkedIn talk together. We're about to release it's all about that, by the way. Everyone needs to get better, ourselves included. It's not a quick fix. Fundamentally, systemically, it needs to be integrated to every organization because the data shows that the more diverse and inclusive a company, the higher the profitability of the company. Its fact-based across industry. There are so many studies that have been done, but it has to start fundamentally out of college, too, and access programs where there's the ability to go work for suppliers and distributors. By the way, there's great work being done right now, it just takes real collaboration throughout the industry to do it because it has been without a lot of duplicity in the past, it's getting better every day, but you can't rest. You have to continue do it. We brought in someone in our organization just to work with on diversity and inclusion with US. We have to practice what we preach, and we have to figure out a better way for the next 20 years to grow an organization. And by the way, these companies, these wine companies, spirits companies, food companies, beauty companies, cannabis, they're coming to us asking us how to do it. So, there's an ecosystem to support it. I would say Women of the Vine and Spirits has done a great job with it. Be the change did a great job with the job fair they did. But the work continues, and I do believe that we'll get there. I'm really optimistic and we find ourselves in a really valuable seat to influence and connect, and it's a big part of the future.

SR: The question I asked was we were in an industry that was not very diverse. And you say you are seeing that change. Is that different, or is the speed of change, the rate of change different for suppliers, domestic or international, or for importers or for distributors or retailers or service companies?

JW: I think it's across the board, man. If you look at all the venture capital and private equity coming into our space, we deal with most of them. They don't want to invest in companies unless there's a diverse board. They want to know that there's real diversity in the organization. It's a mandate.

The board dictates the growth trajectory in conjunction with the CEO and the COO and CFO of the company to build an organization that consists of, like, collaborative, diverse opinions so they can really go successfully position themselves in the market. The more diverse the board, the higher the likelihood that you will have real value propositions in the market and run a company in a healthy way. The Nasdaq just announced this diversity in boards, this bill that's passing. Nothing happens overnight, but every little bit matters, and no one can avoid it. It's critically important, and we've got to educate the younger generation on how wonderful this industry is. Ten years ago, 15 years ago, you go to a job fair on a career campus. You might see a distributor; you might see Red Bull. No one was recruiting. That's changing systemically at the point of career journey, these organizations are going deep in, and they are making sure that they have really wonderful talent acquisition, organizational design, like human resources, thought leaders to be choiceful about how they grow, the future state of the business in the way they recruit. It is changing, because we hear it all the time, it's going to have to be a constant evolution and nothing's overnight, but I feel really optimistic about where we're heading.

SR: How can someone differentiate themselves or be recognized in a world of digital evaluation and online communication?

JW: Good old-fashioned courtesy, gratitude and thoughtful outreach?
SR: I've known Josh for a long time. We hadn't spoken probably in a year. One day I got a handwritten note in the mail saying, hey Steve, we haven't spoken for a while, let's get on the phone together. I got to say, my world stopped. I mean, that kind of stuff used to happen. We used to write letters in the days before FedEx, but that was so unique and so differentiating. Are people doing that or what are some variations on that that they may be doing that may be digital?
JW: Yes. I still to this day, write 15 thank you cards a week, probably. I mainly do it because I enjoy it. I can't tell you how many CEOs and founders, I couldn't even count it, dozens and dozens have written me thank you cards, thanking me for the thank you card.
SR: All right. When does it stop?
JW: You name it! All the way to the top. Email has become so obligatory, and we get bombarded by emails and everyone's pitching you on something. Nine times out of ten, people don't even send a follow up thank you. Sometimes they do. Gratitude matters. If you are a human being that wants to persuade an organization to bring you on to join that specific organization, you have a much higher likelihood and probability of being asked to join the organization. If you have some type of compelling communication style. What do I mean by that? I get LinkedIn requests all the time. I don't even have time to respond to all the requests. But when I get a message from someone on LinkedIn or an email that

expresses how much they respect our organization and what we're about and exactly what we do, and quote a specific comment on an interview or talk to me about one area in my career or someone that they know that I know in the industry who they respect a great deal, who they had a conversation with, by the way, everyone knows someone that knows someone. That's why LinkedIn connections exist, right. If you're thoughtful in the way you do that in a fun, professional, thought-provoking way, anyone's going to respond. And you know what? If you get the attention of a CEO or VP of finance or VP of sales, man, I really liked that person. If they respond, they're going to say, well, that's something that could really add value to course we're going to let them talk to our team, because they're not robots and just sending pieces of paper and resumes out everywhere.

SR: One of the issues that I see coming up is salary expectations being out of sync for a lot of younger kids. Can you talk about salary expectations and job responsibilities and inflation in there?

JW: Probably the most challenging conversation right now. You read about it across the value chain. There's a shortage of labor. Starting at retail to college graduates, to mid-level management to director and VPs. Salary and compensation expectations have shifted so significantly. At the beginning of the COVID-19 we were just grateful to have a job like, thank God we're employed, and we can feed our family, right. A lot of people post-COVID as we get to the tail end. I've never seen comp structures look like they do now. So much money is hitting the private markets right now through investment, through venture and private equity, especially in consumer, consumer, tech. Anything you'd order on Amazon, right. Anything you'd order on Drizly. There's so much funding and valuations are so frothy that with that comes the ability and a healthy balance sheet to pay compensation packages and structures that were 20-30% what they were a year ago, and the tech industry is not helping with that, because when you look at, you look at where our business is shifting and the fundamental kind of like evolution is DTC and e-commerce. Right. I mean, that's where it's really technology integration. Where do those people come from? Silicon Valley. Silicon Valley. Right. Complex issues. What type of companies that work for injuries and back companies, Sequoia-backed companies. Bessemer-backed companies. Because guess who's investing in these bev-tech companies. So, with that comes an imbalance. What I mean is, if all the tech talent is going to make this much, then there's got to be parity. Why wouldn't the traditional sales talent make this much? Why wouldn't operations talent make this much? Why wouldn't finance talent make this much? Because these are high growth companies that are very well backed. Even the public companies, the public beverage - alcohol companies, they cannot keep people employed because people are leaving for more money. They're saying, what do you mean? We always have compensation committees. We always have these bands. It's kind of out the window right now. It's to a point where it's really hard because there has to be a course correction in the economy in general where competition has to be in line with contribution and skill set. There was a misalignment where in a lot of areas, people weren't being paid what they were in other adjacent industries for the same role. That's changed. It will continue to. It's going to be interesting to see how much volume is driven omnichannel together and what type of talent. You see the big suppliers and distributors investing so much in technology and engineering and product. There's going to be a lot of specialization in the field. It will enable salespeople to be much more powerful actually.

SR: One of the things I'd like to end with the big takeaway. What's something that everybody can take away from what we just talked about, put to use immediately and improve their own situation, whether it's a job, not necessarily a job search, but in the way they conduct themselves in business and so forth.

SR: Yeah. For me, it's simply do what you love, know what you're good at, and double down there. If you're making a step in your career, find a company that's meaningful to you and have a clear idea of actually what you would enjoy doing. There's no shame in figuring out what you would enjoy doing. If it's sales, if it's marketing, if it's operations, if it's making things, production, all these companies, they do all of that. They literally do all of that. So, figure it out what it is or the type of organization in an industry or the type of sector that aligns with your values and excites you and find the people in that company that run that department and do that job and respectfully and thoughtfully and humbly reach out to them in an engaging way to find out more. If you're a senior level exec and you've just gone through the pandemic and you're the stage in your career where you've been able to reevaluate life and gain perspective, do what you love there, too. Life is too short. Join a company that matters. If you've always wanted to be with a high growth private equity backed company and build and sell it like a Deep Eddie, then go join a company like that. If you've always wanted to work for a global CPG, go do it. But if you don't take the steps to go do it, no one can do it for you. There is a big demand for talented people at all levels right now. There are more jobs than I've ever seen. Ever. And there's going to be no slowdown, I believe, in the next twelve to 18 months. So now is the time to kind of dig deep and figure out what you want to do and go find it, because no one else is going to make it happen.

The takeaway

> **"Increase diversity and inclusivity in the workplace to improve the bottom line. Do what you love. Gratitude matters."**

Conversation XXI

EPISODE 659 –DEBORAH BRENNER

The audio

The issues

Diversity, equity and inclusion in the workplace.

The guest

Deborah Brenner is the Founder & CEO of Women of the Vine & Spirits, a membership organization dedicated to promoting diversity, equality and inclusion in the wine, beer and spirits industry. She is also the President of the Women of the Vine & Spirits Foundation, which provides scholarships to help women advance their careers in the food, wine, spirits, beer and hospitality industries through education, leadership and professional development.

The conversation

DB: I'm a reinvention story and I've met many people recently and especially that are transitioning their careers. I spent almost 20 years in the technology sector. I worked with high end technology used in television and film studios, but it was a very male dominated industry. I joined it in the late eighties, and it was a fascinating and wonderful industry, but I really felt that I was hitting a lot of barriers and got quite frustrated. Especially back then, there were no female role models and very few women being promoted, so I decided to reinvent myself and pursue my passion in the wine industry. During a trip and learning about the different winemakers, I was amazed to find out all the women that were behind some of the iconic brands that consumers are bringing to their table and enjoying at restaurants every day and have no idea that women were behind them. That is what compelled me to tell their stories and write the book *Women of the Vine*, inside the world of women who make, taste and enjoy wine. Believe it or not, Steve, this October we are celebrating the 15th anniversary since I wrote that book.

SR: Congratulations! As a fellow author, I know how challenging that is. How current do you think the book is 15 years on?

DB: Well, I think it's quite current in that a lot of the barriers that I talk about. It was one of the first books to really talk about championing women and recognizing women that were quite underrecognized in this industry, even 15 years later, where we sit today. This has really been the catalyst for me to create the year-round global organization, Women of the Vine & Spirits, which I am founder and CEO today. As you point out, Steve, what's changed? Well, some things have changed, but a lot has not. There's a lot of progress that we need to do to make the beverage/alcohol industry more diverse, more equitable and more inclusive, and that's now 15 years later. Not just because it's a good

thing to do, but it's now become a business imperative.
SR: Explain that a little bit more, because globally there's been a complete sea change in attitude and appreciation of that, certainly here in the United States. It has always been a good thing, but now it has become front and center. So, talk about that.
DB: Absolutely. The wine and spirits and beer industry is one of the oldest globally traded industries. You look at the history of humanity, there was a way that wine and spirits and beer was marketed for quite a long time, decade after decade. Now what's happening is that we're seeing the consumer changing. The census data recently that just came out really demonstrated that, in the United States in particular. Minorities are no longer the minority - they are the majority. So, it's becoming a business imperative for companies in beverage/alcohol and in all other industries in order to stay competitive, to be creative, to be innovative, and to provide what the consumer is seeking out of their products and brands, you really need to have a diverse and inclusive workforce or you're going to miss out on those opportunities. If everybody looks like me and has my background, that that team isn't going to necessarily be able to innovate across our diverse customer sector. So, it's really important today to stay relevant and competitive.
SR: You use the phrase diversity, equity, inclusion (DEI) Can you define those things?
DB: Absolutely. There's a lot of confusion between equity and equality, right? Diversity, to start off, is basically making sure that you have people in your workforce that represent all different sectors, and that is going to

be people of color, LGBTQ plus IA (intersex and a sexual), and it also includes people with disabilities. Another important thing is neurodiversity, so on the autism spectrum. They say one in six of your employees probably have some sort of ADHD or OCD or Dyslexia. These could be superpowers that they can bring such creativity. We talk about disability, we talk about veterans, like I mentioned, minority, API, Asian Pacific Islanders. It's really important for diversity that you really look at your employee base and your senior leadership to make sure that you have representation, because that leads to the creativity and the innovation. There's a big difference between equity and equality. Equality means that everybody is the same and everybody gets the same. Equality is absolutely the end game, but equity is how we achieve it, and equity is where you have to recognize that not everybody has the same opportunities as others. For example, Women of the Vine and Spirits also have a 501(c)(3) [non-profit, tax-exempt status], and we're about to award over 50 scholarships for education. That is the equity side, right. Not everybody has the financial wherewithal to take a WSET levels 1, 2, 3, 4. It's quite expensive to take the Italian course to be an expert in Italian wine. Equity is where you have to look if you want to help diversify the industry. Are there minorities and groups that don't have the same opportunities? Maybe they don't have a four-year college degree. Maybe you need to look at your hiring and your job postings. Do you really need a four-year college degree? Maybe some of those groups, they didn't have the privilege, they had to go out and work. Those are the kinds of things. Do you have to require somebody to lift 50 pounds when you have forklifts and other things? These are things that we talk a lot about to raise awareness. How's your hiring practice? And the equity side is giving those people the opportunity, either by scholarships, by providing other tools, like in the case of ADHD, sometimes it's as little as noise cancelling headphones so that they can better focus. We do workshops on that. It's fascinating to see just the little tools that can set people up for success with the creativity that they bring. Then Steve, the real magic happens with inclusivity, right? You can go ahead and you can hire people at all different levels of the organization, but if you don't create a culture of inclusivity where they feel they could bring their full, authentic self to work, you're not going to retain those employees because they're going to quickly realize that they don't fit in, that they may not feel like they belong or that people really don't care to hear their opinions or their ideas.

SR: Let's go back to 2015, which was another watershed year in this whole subject, which was your first conference. This, I think, really evolved out of some travel and conversations you had with women wine makers on the West Coast.

DB: Yes, absolutely. Actually, across the United States and even internationally. My personal journey from technology into wine started in New York City, when the Italian Trade Commission was holding an event for people to come and see all different products. I met a young group from Catania, a consortium of wine makers, and they were asking, to your point, the route to market in the United States. At that time, I was working freelance for Cinecittà Studios and I said, well I do marketing and I'm bringing business to Cinecittà Studios in Rome, maybe I can help you understand the route to market in wine in the US. That was the very first step that got me on my journey. They say all roads lead to Rome. That's what led me to start doing my research and going out and realizing the women. So, to your question, it wasn't just women in the US, it was women all over. Over the years, I worked in many capacities in the wine industry myself, from wholesaler, retailer, supplier and consultant. In 2014, I realized there was a huge void. There was an opportunity for the industry as a whole, across all three tiers, to start looking at diversity, equity and inclusion as a whole. As the Woman of the Vine author and being out in the field, realizing that the majority of our wine drinkers, 67% on premise wine drinkers were female, 71% off premise were female, and I'm thinking, oh my gosh, where are the women in leadership, decision-making roles if you want to attract the female consumer? That means all women, women of color, LGBTQ, I put everybody under the big umbrella of women. That's what led me to create the first global symposium.

SR: The first global symposium happened in 2015. Give us a summary of what that was all about, what kind of people came and how it was the genesis of so much to follow.

DB: Well, I was a little bit premature to market. In 2015, DEI wasn't mainstream as a topic the way that it is today. I thought, oh my God, is this going to work? Are people going to come? Am I going to be able to support this financially? I had to rent a venue and I had to have speakers and everything that comes with it. I prayed that I could get 250 attendees to start. We doubled that and sold out. I can tell you that it quickly snowballed from a one-time event into becoming a year-round organization. You could just feel the energy in the room because it was so positive, so uplifting, for the first time we were filling a void where we were coming together, not just women talking to other women, which we've done for decade after decade after decade, but we were there with the men, with the male senior leader having these discussions. The men wanted to have these discussions because they knew that the female consumer had to be addressed, had to be heard. It was an amazing time that we were able to take off our competitive hats across all three tiers and start having conversations for the greater good of the cause.

SR: You made some significant connections from people who either attended or were connected with it in some way. Tell us about a couple of those people who you met.

DB: Well, the first thing that I did, because I had been in the industry for over a decade when I decided that I was going to finance this and try to put together this conference, I called two people that I had known for many years in the industry, Steve Slater and Mel Dick from Southern. At that time, it was Southern Wine and Spirits, now Southern Glazer's. I just thought, okay tell me if this is a really bad idea, because you've seen it all, you've been in the industry. I mean, Mel Dick is an icon.

I was like, tell me this is a bad idea because I don't want to lose my shirt on it. They immediately said, we're behind you, this is important, we have to do this. That's how Southern really came on as one of our first corporate members to get behind the concept. From there, Ste. Michelle Wine Estates and Moët Hennessy were some of the very first that came on board and said, okay we'll get behind you. The first year, 2015, believe it or not, was only wine. The conference was "Women of the Vine". After that, senior figures from Bacardi and Beam Suntory and Brown-Forman saw what we were doing and approached me, hey what about spirits? In 2016 we immediately expanded with Women in the Vine and Spirits. Today I'm extremely proud that we have some major beer companies, because if we're going to really look at creating systemic change of an industry, we need all parties, everybody, to have a seat at the table.

SR: One of the things you had told me was a story about Mel Dick and how his eyes really opened to this subject related to the conference. Can you tell that again for our listeners?

DB: Absolutely. So, again, talk about being early to market! I wrote a book, Woman of the Vine, and I got published 15 years ago, right? It was 2006 and I'm talking about not the wine and their scores from Robert Parker, I'm talking about these women and their gender stereotypes and their barriers and how they're working in a male dominated industry, so it was a little bit before time. Through a family friend who knew Mel Dick, Mel was kind enough to say, okay I'll meet with her in New York. I drove to the city, I don't even think I sat down. I met Mel for the first time, I'm holding my book in my hand and I'm telling him why I think this is important. He immediately picks up his cell phone and he says, I'm sitting here with this "Heimischer" girl and she's onto something. I'm sending her down to your office. He looked at me and he said, kid get in a taxi, you're going to meet Marvin Shanken. Of course, I don't know if I have to say who Marvin is, but for any of the listeners out there who don't, he is the Wine Spectator. Mel was always before his time. He not only started the Wine Division, but he was also the one who created wine by the glass. I mean, you used to have to go to a restaurant and order a bottle. He realized, wait a second, people have different palates, different tastes. So, when he recognized right there that there was something, that was just incredible. Of course, I jumped in the taxi, and I called my parents, I'm Jewish but I don't know Yiddish, and I said, what does Heimischer mean? They said it's a good thing because they knew I was meeting Mel Dick. It's a kind endearing, very charming adjective for a young woman, so it was a really good thing. I went down and I met Marvin and a year later Wine Spectator featured the book in their top 100 reads. From there, I've met the most incredible women. Stephanie Gallo in my book, Gina Gallo wrote the foreword for the book. These were icons and, to me, these were the celebrities of the vine that I was meeting. It's just been incredible around the world that women have been writing to me and involved with us, just really being proud of the work and the contributions and women that trailblazed and really opened the doors for women today in this industry.

SR: Tell us about the current status of Women of the Vine and the programs that you're involved in.

DB: Absolutely. From the first global symposium being a two-and-a-half-day event, as I mentioned, I quickly realized that to create change, you can't just gather once a year and have a conversation. This has to be top of mind and ongoing conversation 365 days a year. We have to work at a corporate level. We also have to work at an individual level to create change. So, Women in Vine and Spirits, our main pillar is to connect, to collaborate, to make some commitments and take action. All the programs that we do are based on educating both the individual and the corporation, from professional development and personal development to best practices, to looking at what other companies are doing, because everybody is in a different place on the timeline of their DEI journey. We have companies like E. & J. Gallo Winery that really has made great strides for years. They have their employee resource groups and they're doing some amazing work. You have Beam Suntory doing some great work and Brown-Forman with their grow program. You have other companies that are just starting on their DEI journey. One of the most important things that we do is bring together resources and live chats and roundtables and discussions so that everybody can take information back to their company and for themselves of how we all could be a part of the change. Then the other thing that we do is we bring experts in from outside of our industry to share their expertise, to be able to guide companies. Not everybody can afford to have consultants to come in and guide your company on how to set up a DEI council, how to set up employee research groups or business resource groups. They can get that at Women of the Vine and Spirits as well. The other thing that they get is the benefit of DEI is what I call BD&I, and that's business development and innovation. We constantly prove what the studies show is that DEI leads to creativity, innovation, and a greater bottom line. So networking and current trends in sales and everything, how to move product to e-commerce, that's all-important stuff because economic empowerment is the pathway to equality.

SR: It's all about conversation and certainly not platitudes and certainly not written four points or those kinds of things. How do you stimulate that kind of dialogue now that we're going to at some point in time, if not the end of COVID, whatever, the next phase is going to be where commerce again takes off. Where is Women of the Vine and Spirits going to go in the post COVID world?

DB: Well, I think the beauty that we realized and thank goodness for technology and talk about innovation and quickly pivoting, is that we realized that with the technology we had, we no longer had the travel restrictions and the geographic barriers. We truly could come together on a global scale using the technology and Zoom to really be able to network for business development and to drive DEI changes. Post-COVID, we're in a very social industry of beverage-alcohol, right. We want to get together and have dinner and have a cocktail and share. That will never change. We can't wait until we can get back together in person. The one thing that we realized is that in a 30- or 60-minute Zoom we can accomplish so much and we can bring so much diversity of thought together that we couldn't do getting on airplanes and coming. The world has switched and for Women in the Vine and Spirits, the hybrid mode is definitely where we're going to be going so that we can stay well connected all the time and across all kinds of not just geographic barriers, but also time zones. There's a lot of good things that are coming from this. It's also allowed us to meet one another more than we ever have. I've met more of our members and more people of the wine, beer and spirits community because I didn't have all of the travel time. That's really very positive. We're going to see a lot of the things that change, like e-commerce, Drizly with delivery, ReserveBar's doing what they're doing, ready to drink cocktails is explosive. These things, I think, are here to stay. We want more and more people to engage, because when you're trying to create systemic change in an industry, we're stronger together when we amplify each other's voice.

SR: We've talked about a lot of programs that you guys have and the goals and how to enhance communication. Of some of those things that we talked about, what can people put to use immediately based on what we just discussed here at this, beyond just going to your website, is there something in your mind?

DB: Absolutely. I think the big takeaway that I'd like people is that change starts with one person at a time. It starts at the individual level. It's a personal journey as you start looking at this and awareness is the very first thing is to start becoming aware. Look for those teachable moments and just take a moment to listen and to learn. Just listen, hear how people are speaking about this subject of DEI. I take them as these teachable moments and question yourself about where some of your own biases lie, because we all have biases, it's part of human nature. That's the first step, becoming aware and then having the opportunity to learn and ask questions and be willing to be open to understand it. The next thing is from that, don't be afraid to use your voice to champion change, because if you're in a leadership position, then you're in a really good position to talk to your company about change. But if you're an individual and you're not in a leadership, you still can create change within your peer sector by being able to use your voice. Sometimes using your voice just means asking people to just listen. That's really the most important takeaway, to get personally involved, because when you think about how many people are involved in beverage -alcohol, if everybody just took a moment to become more aware, as McKinsey says in their studies, they're saying it could take 100 years to actually reach gender equality. I won't be alive. I'm hoping we all band together, amplify our voices and accelerate the pace.

The takeaway

> **"With changing demographics and societal expectations, increasing diversity, equity and inclusion in the workplace is not just the right thing to do, but a business imperative."**

Conversation XXII

EPISODE 823 – DON KAVANAGH

The audio

The issues

Technology, breaking into new markets, consumer access, price transparency and how small brands can compete

The guest

Don Kavanagh is the editor of Wine-Searcher, a search engine and app that enables users to locate the price and availability of a given wine, whiskey, spirit or beer globally, and be directed to a relevant retailer. He has spent the past 25 years either working in the wine trade or writing about it, in his native Ireland, the UK, and New Zealand, at various times a wine merchant, bartender, moonshiner, magazine editor and news journalist.

The conversation

SR: Tell us a little bit about what Wine-Searcher is, what are your functions.

DK: Basically, Wine-Searcher is a wine search engine. What we do is we gather prices from thousands of retailers around the world and we display them so people can make better buying decisions. Know more, pay less.

SR: Your target audience is it the trade or consumers or what did it start out with and what has it morphed into?

DK: It started out as a trade tool. It started out way back in 1996, I believe. When our CEO, Martin Brown, he got the idea when he was working for Berry Brothers and Rudd, the great old venerable merchants in London. He was part of their IT team and rather than having people manually checking prices that their competitors were charging for various wines, he came up with a way of doing it automatically, and Wine-Searcher was born. A couple of years later, he moved back to New Zealand and we've been based here ever since.

SR: And the monetization of that? My understanding is the retailers pay to have their products checked and listed.

DK: Yes. They don't have to. Many of them do. Many of them choose to. They become sponsors, which means they get a little bit more promotion, they're more visible. Their entries will be in bold rather than in standard type. If somebody clicks through to the merchant website, then we clip that part of the ticket and that's it. We don't take any money from sales, but we take a tiny amount for a referral.

SR: Transparency of pricing is one of the fundamental principles that you guys are working with. I know working on the side of the business that I am for a lot of especially higher end wineries that we work with, they're less enthralled with Wine-Searcher than other people are because they feel that it can undermine the MSRP, the Manufacturers Suggested Retail Price of

their product, either because of the way it's displayed in Wine-Searcher or the way you can rank it. Can you talk about that challenge of how you guys have accuracy in prices and this whole issue? A lot of people say that the stuff on Wine-Searcher often includes people who are faking prices just to manipulate the system.
DK: Well, if people are faking prices to manipulate their ranking in our results, people tend to let us know. If that happens, then we deal with that merchant and we explain the rules to them that prices must be, unless otherwise stated, for in stock wine. Basically, they have to have the wine on hand and available at that price for them to be able to put that price on a wine.
SR: Beyond pricing, you guys provide a lot more information, ratings, reviews, regional profiles, etc. Talk about the rest of the non-pricing information that's available on Wine-Searcher and what role that plays.
DK: Well, this is the thing about Wine-Searcher, it's this great undiscovered treasure trove of information. It's not just pricing. I know a lot of people just use it for pricing, but our encyclopedia is huge. It's genuinely, and I'm not just saying this because I'm the editor, one of the best wine resources available online.
We go from the very basics of France as a wine region down through to lieu-dit in Burgundy. We've literally got every AVA that's ever been made. We've got every appellation in France. We've got every tiny little subregion of Italy or anywhere where they make wine. We've got entries on Tahiti. We have entries on Nigeria, not places that you'd automatically think of for wine.
SR: So how do you get that information? How does

that get populated into the database?

DK: That gets populated by an awful lot of hard work, by an awful lot of dedicated people. We currently have a team of six and we basically look after the encyclopedia. Then there's another wine specialist team that looks after things like the scores, the awards, the critics, and so forth.

What we do is we refine all that so that eventually any combination of that name that you put in will eventually arrive at the destination of the wine you're looking for. There's the wine specialist team and the content team, who do all the writing, basically. We've written not just us, the current team, but down the years, there have been stalwarts, people just typing away, writing all that stuff, and we get a lot of information from the appellations themselves, from existing wine encyclopedias and from our knowledge - we're quite a knowledgeable bunch.

SR: So, if you're from a *consorzio* in Italy or a winery in Chile or whatever, and they see information that are lacking or information that's incorrect or needs to be updated, how can individuals who are in the business optimize, correct, provide updated information and assets, including visuals and so forth to you guys?

DK: Simple. They can just email us. We've got a contact us Wine-Searcher section. Just hit the automatic email, tell us what the issue is, and we'll be back to you pretty much straight away.

SR: How do you do that with six people? Is any of it automated so that content is scraped, or is somebody, a human, always looking at it?

DK: There's always a human looking at it.

SR: Wow! I don't think people recognize that about Wine-Searcher.

DK: No, I don't think they do either. It's the old swan analogy. We're sailing along beautifully on top of the water and paddling furiously underneath where nobody can see. I'm incredibly proud of what we've got. As I said, our encyclopedia, the regions, the grape varieties, the producer profiles that we're constantly writing new ones of. We've got 4000 producer profiles on there already, and we're pumping out more each month. Of course, the job is getting bigger as well. We're improving the amount of information associated with each wine as well. We're getting technical sheets from the producers themselves. Eventually what we're moving towards is being able to provide full technical information, down to grams per liter of residual sugar, harvest dates for each wine, whether they're vegan wines and so forth. Eventually people will be able to search by that. People will be able to search by white wine, Riesling, less than seven grams of residual sugar, and then for by country or by producer or whatever, if they want to. We've got a lot of work on. We're making it broader and deeper, and it's a spectacular resource, just horrifically underused, I believe.

SR: My philosophy is that most people want to know just two things about a wine: what does it taste like in words that I understand and is it going to go with whatever it is that I'm making for dinner tonight? Anything beyond that and we're talking to ourselves, and maybe that's a negative. Why do you do high-end roundups as opposed to focusing on the wines that

people can buy?
DK: We can do that. The reason we do the ones that we do is that's a bit of fun, really. These are aspirational searches in 90% of the cases, although at times actual wines that people are looking for that are not necessarily the esoteric, they're not the Henri Jayer, they're not Chateaux Lafite, they're not Screaming Eagle Sauvignon Blanc. Sometimes wines will break through into it, wines and indeed whiskies, will break through. Blanton's Bourbon, for example, was in the top ten for over a year, was in our most searched for products for more than a year at one stage, which wasn't bad for a $50 bottle of bourbon. But with the stories themselves, they're a bit of fun, really, because they genuinely are what people are using our website to search for, whether or not they have any value to the trade I would doubt. They make for a pleasant four or five minutes of somebody reading something on their phone while they're on the subway. It's fun and they're incredibly popular. We get a lot of readers.

SR: I remember the days of when when nobody really had a good idea of what prices were actually being charged. Now, all of a sudden, you've made that information available, along with the qualitative information that supports that on the regions, the wineries, the histories, the people who make it and all that kind of stuff What's coming down the pipe in terms of services and capabilities for Wine-Searcher?

DK: Well, basically, it's more and better. We're going to offer more information. We want to be a tool that informs the user all the way through the transaction.

From the decision-making process at the start of which wine I want to buy and why I want to buy it through to the where do I buy it, how can I get it delivered to me and so forth? That's coming. We do a lot of it already, but the idea is to present more information. We've got more tech sheets from producers and so forth. We're going to be able to offer full technical specifications for every single wine on the site.

SR: When we're talking about critics, reviews, are there any critics that you don't include?

DK: Oh, there's lots. We've really only got the top 40. They're the ones that we feel are authoritative enough and credible enough. Often, we'll get irate emails from some producer somewhere. It says, excuse me, my 1998 vintage of my Malbec scored 99 at the Outer Mongolia regional wine show, so why have I only got an aggregated score of 88 for that wine? It's because we look for authoritative, credible critics. So, you know, the Jancis Robinsons, the Wine Advocates of the world, the Wine Spectators of the world, the Wine Enthusiasts of the world, Cellar Tracker, people like that, and some fairly specific ones, too, for Italy, in Germany and Spain and so forth.

SR: We've covered a lot of ground here, I appreciate your time. What is the big takeaway, someone who is listening to this, and most of my listeners are in the trade and predominantly in the US, UK and Italy, that somebody could put to use immediately from your perspective of what we just discussed?

DK: Well, the big thing is there's more to us than you think. We're not just a search engine. We offer everything from vintage charts going back to early 1900s with descriptions of the vintages of each, everywhere in every little region in the world. We've got that, where we put all that together in one place for people. We've got all the information you could possibly need to educate your consumers and to educate your staff about the wines they're selling. As we go along, we get bigger. We end up with more information all the time. If it's information you want, we've got it. We're the only people who can measure demand for wines.

The takeaway

> **"New technology, like find and compare search engines, are a valuable tool for the trade and consumers alike, and can enable brands to optimize their online presence at low cost."**

The takeaways

I. Create community and empower employees to lead innovation within the workplace.

II. Be a strong voice for change and provide tangible opportunities to minority communities through scholarships, partnerships and mentoring.

III. Stimulate the market and reinvent the appeal of traditional wine products through innovation, while encouraging new discussions of wine's place alongside emerging products.

IV. Understand the significant barriers that continue to exist in sectors of the wine world, build strategies to surmount them; recognize the diverse range of cultural reference points held by consumers and producers alike.

V. Physical disability should not exclude anyone from wine. Teams with greater diversity are more effective and can positively impact the bottom line.

VI. Creating barrier free spaces is more than just a design issue, it must be accompanied by a culture of empathy. Entrepreneurs should be spokespeople for inclusion and education inside and outside their professional spaces.

VII. Recognize the barriers created by racism and elitism and encourage and support removing those barriers through education, innovation and opportunity.

VIII. Support policies and encourage businesses who are engaged in the conservation and preservation of vulnerable ecosystems and historic viticultural practices.

IX. Recognize the value of co-operatives for maintaining the economic, social and environmental viability of rural communities.

X. Ancient cultures, like ancient vines, need to be carefully nurtured to prepare them for the future, blending tradition with innovation and technology.

XI. Respect the contribution of previous generations and the social and political context in which they built the foundations of today's viticulture. New generations can build on those foundations to create a more sustainable future for viticulture.

XII. The future can sometimes be found in the past, as experience and farming methods based on respect for the land and the soil are rediscovered, offering sustainable solutions and attracting younger people back to rural communities.

XIII. Focus on the power and creativity of women to produce great things, and their ability to connect history, culture, art and wine.

XIV. Offer a service that is authentic and empathetic.

XV. Marginalized groups have much to offer. Empower those who have been marginalized and communicate through demonstration.

XVI. Create non-judgmental spaces and use language that reflects a diversity of backgrounds and cultural reference points.

XVII. Embrace new technology that has opened up direct-to-consumer channels that allow producers to manage and build their brand online.

XVIII. Foster partnerships with relevant stakeholders to understand and gain access to complex liquor markets.

XIX. New technology can allow smaller producers to engage directly with consumers in a meaningful and profitable way.

XX. Increase diversity and inclusivity in the workplace to improve the bottom line. Do what you love. Gratitude matters.

XXI. With changing demographics and societal expectations, increasing diversity, equity and inclusion in the workplace is not just the right thing to do, but a business imperative.

XXII. New technology, like find and compare search engines, are a valuable tool for the trade and consumers alike, and can enable brands to optimize their online presence at low cost.

LEARN MORE ABOUT ITALIAN WINES WITH OUR BOOKS

COMING SOON

If this book has inspired and encouraged you to learn more about Italian wines, you may also wish to consider some of these other publications that come highly recommended! Here's a sneak preview of what's coming soon! Find out more at mammajumboshrimp.com

Master of Wine - Tre storie in un viaggio

The individual stories of Andrea Lonardi, Gabriele Gorelli and Pietro Russo converge and merge in the journey the three took to become Masters of Wine.
The results are unprecedented: several Italians before them have taken the same path, but no one has ever achieved the ultimate goal. Why, with 498 MW from over 30 countries in almost 70 years, has Italy been absent from the picture until recently? Why exactly did these three Italians manage to become a joint voice raised above the chorus? Perhaps the key lies precisely in their three stories; indeed, in their shared history.

Italian Wine Unplugged 2.0

Following on from our first edition published in 2017, 2.0 as it's fondly known, is the result of a communi-

ty-wide project, proving once again that the best things need a village for the growth process. We pulled apart a book we loved, and then we rewrote, reshaped and re-directed the direction of what has become the cornerstone of our wine education program. Covering all the Italian native grapes, adding sections on breakthroughs in soil and DNA analysis, seasoning with history, food pairings, and benchmark producers, we expanded and streamlined this invaluable tool for those who want to dig deep into Italian wine knowledge. Italian Wine Unplugged 2.0 is the most up to date and comprehensive study guide available for all Italian wine lovers.

BACK CATALOGUE

Italian Wine Unplugged

A comprehensive cultural and scientific introduction to Italian wines and its hundreds of native grapes. The formation is organised in accessible, color-coded and easy-to-read entries. www.italianwineunplugged.com.

Sangiovese, Lambrusco, and Other Vine Stories

These stories explore the cultivation of grapevines, along with the history of human communities that influenced the production and trading of Italian wines. It follows the lineage of wine through a discussion of the origin and ancestry of vines such as Sangiovese, Ribolla, Primitivo and the many Moscato, Malvasia, and Lambrusco grapes.

#nofilter: 12 Q&A with Italian Wine Influencers

This book gives a snapshot of wine influencer scene in Italy. It is a collection of interviews with 9 Italian wine influencers who openly discuss their work and love for wine. They provide tips on becoming an influencer and share advice on how wineries can harness the potential of social media.

Jumbo Shrimp Guide to Italian Wine

Sometimes it's nice to learn about the wine you are sipping with ease and pleasure. However, talking about Italian wine is not always easy and broaching the grape varieties, the wines and the history can be daunting, especially if you are looking for a quick fix that can explain the complexities of this world. The book offers all the tools to easily remember the key elements: how to read and understand the labels, the geographical information underlying each wine, the various types of grapes, and the most significant wines that could act as representatives of what is likely the most varied and qualitative wine production model in the world.

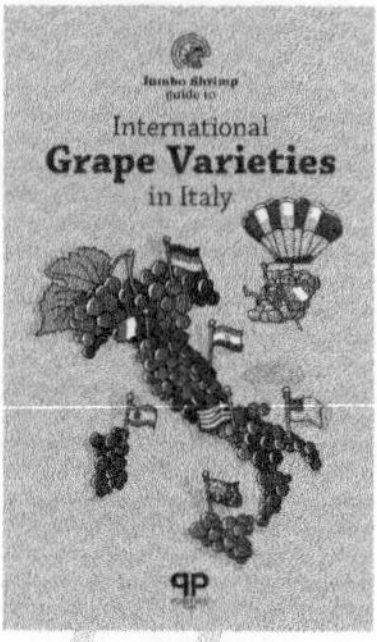

The Jumbo Shrimp Guide to International Grape Varieties in Italy

The book was created thanks to the collaboration between three writers that realized that in the current trend towards more and more obscure varieties, and the hunt for the lesser known wines, many great grapes, denominations and wines are overlooked in new literature about Italian wine. It's true that Italy has more than 500 nationally registered native grapes, but it's also true that in many regions of Italy some of the best wines are made using international varieties.

OTHER RESOURCES

ITALIAN WINE PODCAST

The Italian Wine Podcast began as a storytelling project dedicated to the Italian wine world. It started in March 2017 in the lead-up to major Italian wine events: OperaWine and Vinitaly, and has since become an award-winning show, recognized as one of the most frequently listened-to wine podcasts out there. Italy has more native grape varieties concentrated within its borders than any other country in the world, and Italian wine and grape diversity is a story worth telling. Meanwhile, the popularity of Italian wine continues to grow on an international scale, so, despite its name, the shows are equally geared towards the international wine community. The Italian Wine Podcast aims to inform, educate, and entertain fans through engaging conversations with producers, experts, and personalities of the Italian and international wine scene.
(www.italianwinepodcast.com)

VINITALY INTERNATIONAL ACADEMY

Vinitaly International Academy (VIA) aims to be the gold standard of Italian wine education. VIA offers a complete educational path with standardised courses that will teach professionals and educators to master the diversity of Italian wine in a rigorous, organized manner. Find out more at vinitalyinternational.com/vinitaly-international-academy.

MAMMA JUMBO SHRIMP

The Mamma Jumbo Shrimp YouTube Channel is part of the Mamma Jumbo Shrimp family of multi-media wine-related content. In addition to wine, the channel also covers food and travel with regularly updated video content from across the globe. From in-depth on-location interviews with iconic wine producers to fun food and wine tastings, every aspect of Italian wine culture is explored in entertaining and engaging video format.